HAND BOOK

BEFORE YOU START TO READ THIS BOOK, take this moment to think about making a donation to punctum books, an independent non-profit press,

@ https://punctumbooks.com/support/

If you're reading the e-book, you can click on the image below to go directly to our donations site. Any amount, no matter the size, is appreciated and will help us to keep our ship of fools afloat. Contributions from dedicated readers will also help us to keep our commons open and to cultivate new work that can't find a welcoming port elsewhere. Our adventure is not possible without your support.

Vive la Open Access.

Fig. 1. Detail from Hieronymus Bosch, *Ship of Fools* (1490–1500)

HAND BOOK: A MANUAL ON PERFORMANCE, PROCESS, AND THE LABOR OF LAUNDRY. Copyright © 2025 by Lizzie Olesker and Lynne Sachs. This work carries a Creative Commons BY-NC-SA 4.0 International license, which means that you are free to copy and redistribute the material in any medium or format, and you may also remix, transform and build upon the material, as long as you clearly attribute the work to the authors (but not in a way that suggests the authors or punctum books endorses you and your work), you do not use this work for commercial gain in any form whatsoever, and that for any remixing and transformation, you distribute your rebuild under the same license. http://creativecommons.org/licenses/by-nc-sa/4.0/

First published in 2025 by punctum books, Earth, Milky Way.
https://punctumbooks.com

ISBN-13: 978-1-68571-182-5 (print)
ISBN-13: 978-1-68571-183-2 (ePDF)

DOI: 10.53288/0490.1.00

LCCN: 2025938085
Library of Congress Cataloging Data is available from the Library of Congress

Editing: Eileen A. Fradenburg Joy and SAJ
Book design: Hatim Eujayl and Vincent W.J. van Gerven Oei
Cover design: Vincent W.J. van Gerven Oei

HIC SVNT MONSTRA

Lizzie Olesker &
Lynne Sachs

Hand Book

A Manual

on performance,
process, and the
labor of laundry

contents

Foreword: A New Refusal and a New Struggle   15
Silvia Federici

Introduction: Performance, Process, and the Labor of Laundry   19

A Thousand Pieces a Day   27
Margarita Lopez

Lint   29
Lynne Sachs

Finding the Stain: A Transcript in Translation   31
interviews and translations by Luo Xiaoyua

        IN MOTION — A Folding Dance

Score for a Folding Dance   37
composed and performed by Veraalba Santa

        IN MOTION — Transforming through Clothing

Every Fold Matters, a playscript

Taking on a Role   97
Jasmine Holloway

Articles on the Washing Society from *The Atlanta Constitution*, 1881   99

A Hole in History: In Conversation with Tera Hunter   113

        IN MOTION — Lint with Voices

In Praxis: A Bridge between Art and Activism *with Rosana Rodríguez and Mahoma López*	119
IN MOTION — Dancing on Washing Machines	
Shake, Rattle, and… *Stephen Vitiello*	129
Sound of a Machine Door Closing *Amanda Katz*	131
IN MOTION — Two Women Folding	
Service, Not Servitude *Andrea Estepa*	135
Reflections on Laundry and Reproductive Labor: In Conversation with Silvia Federici	139
Aid *Lizzie Olesker*	149
Worry *Lynne Sachs*	151
Questions on Black and White: A Photograph by Gertrude Kasebier	155
Loads of Prose: From the Beginning *Emily Rubin*	161
Reception Theory	163
How It Happened: Performances and Screenings	173
Epilogue	179
Contributors	181
List of Illustrations	185
Acknowledgments	189

for our mothers, Elaine Olesker and Diane Sachs

foreword

A NEW REFUSAL AND
A NEW STRUGGLE

Silvia Federici

The washing of clothes, the laundry, has long been seen as an iconic reproductive activity for women, an occasion for sociality, a time to gather at rivers and streams, around washboards, or amidst the machines in laundromats, all in the collective ritual of bringing dirty clothes back to life. It has also become an inspirational subject for feminist writers and filmmakers.

Hand Book: A Manual on Performance, Process, and the Labor of Laundry continues in part this tradition. The book is, in many ways, a unique work. The variety and richness of the materials, gathered by the authors, is one reason for its originality. Composed in a choral, multilayered way, with voices coming from different places in the laundry world, the book brings together images, interviews with workers and organizers, and accounts of actions that have taken place in recent years in New York City laundromats, all reflecting on the meaning of laundry as an activity and the epochal changes that have taken place in its organization.

The story these workers tell us—powerfully reconstructed by Lizzie Olesker and Lynne Sachs—discloses a world that now remains invisible to those for whom the clothes are washed. And, at the same time, it is a world where (as the authors write) "the private meets the public." Clothes speak, deliver forgotten keys and other objects, and reveal something about their owners' lives. But to the workers, they are also a health threat. Adding to the long hours of work, the miserable pay, and the toxicity of the environment, there is the fear and repugnance that the workers must overcome. They sort through soiled clothes and the recriminations of bossy customers who are ignorant of the hard labor behind the cleaned clothes, often threatening the workers in a classic colonialist way. From *Hand Book*, we also learn that in many areas, the old drop-off laundromat has been replaced, moved to the outskirts of towns, performed by mega machines where workers, predominantly female immigrants, wash and fold thousands of clothes every day, until their bodies ache.

Hand Book demonstrates that despite its "modernity," the laundry remains a place of colonial relations. As with other aspects of domestic work, mechanization has neither improved the conditions of the workers, nor has it put an end to their struggles. It is significant, in this context, that among the materials that Olesker and Sachs have brought together in *Hand Book,* they include a report on the 1881 strike in which Black laundry workers in Atlanta, Georgia organized to demand higher pay. Since the strike was apparently successful, one wonders to what extent such a demonstration of agency, such a decisive refusal of exploitation by a population of women just coming out of slavery, was a factor in the development of the first washing machines in the United States in the second part of the nineteenth century. The relation of art to history, and of art to politics, is one of the themes Olesker and Sachs raise in their questioning. It is a theme that they approach practically as well as theoretically.

The inclusion of an account of the 1881 laundry workers' strike speaks to its historical significance. *Hand Book* strives not only to report but also to intervene in and contribute to the workers' struggle. Here, we also discover the contemporary voices of the leaders from the Laundry Workers Center who today in New York City are fighting for better working conditions and higher pay and whose actions the authors have documented. Appropriately, in this vein *Hand Book* includes images and accounts of a performance and film Olesker and Sachs created as part of their work with laundry workers.

Does art embody a politics? This book demonstrates it can, helping us to move beyond the world of the factual to that of desires, possibilities, and imagined realities. Throughout the book, the stories, reflections, and complaints of laundry workers, along with images portraying the instruments of their work, come together in the metaphorical gesture of lint, making it a symbol of what remains at the end of the workday. In *Hand Book: A Manual,* workers transgress their expected role as "dutiful machines" as they fold hundreds of pieces an hour, then break out, dancing, leaping over the washers and dryers in a sort of war dance, a prelude to a new refusal, and a new struggle.

INTRODUCTION

Performance, Process, and the Labor of Laundry

This is not a play. It is something else.
Call it a blueprint, a map, a documentation
of something that has already happened
but could happen again —
a rendering in book form of a performance.
Making a mark, words on a page instead of bodies in space.
A book that contains what's remembered and what could be.
All of it written down and placed here, into this
Hand Book: A Manual.

We are a playwright and a filmmaker who discovered a shared interest in making work that magnifies quotidian elements of life in the city where we live. We met years ago in Brooklyn while sitting on a bench waiting for our young daughters to finish their music lessons. A conversation began about our lives as mothers and working artists. We couldn't yet know that those early encounters would lead to a ten-year theater and film collaboration. Now in our sixties, our daughters fully grown, we continue to build an experimental model for making live performance and film, engaging in a dialogue on how art-making can alter our understanding of urban life.

Soon after meeting, we attended each other's performance events. Lizzie first saw Lynne's *Your Day is My Night* at Proteus Gowanus, a Brooklyn gallery space on the ground floor of a former factory. Through verité conversations, character-driven fictions, and multi-format film loops, this immersive, interactive one-hour performance conveyed a collective history of seven Chinese immigrants living communally in one simulated "shiftbed" apartment. During the live performance, documentary film footage interrupts choreographed moments where the performers enter, wake up their sleeping housemates, remove their shoes, and climb into a vacated bed. In another area of the gallery space, the actors appear at a table chopping, cooking vegetables, playing cards and giving one another shoulder massages. Spectators become more aware of themselves as voyeuristic observers; they witness the actors transforming into their characters in their own living space. For Lizzie, the entire event opened up questions about what was real and not real, and how everyday gestural actions become elevated in a theatrical context.

When Lynne saw Lizzie's solo "object theater" piece *Infinite Miniature* at Invisible Dog, a converted industrial performance space in Brooklyn, she was immediately struck by the clarity and inventiveness of Lizzie's transformation of a kitchen table into a small-scale stage. With spoons, dishcloth, doll furniture, and thread, she visually represented a mother waiting for her teenage son to return home in the middle of the night. Like a puppeteer, Lizzie manipulated domestic objects that became visual abstractions of the anxiety that emerges from waiting and the cyclical nature of cleaning.

Both of us were ready to shake things up, to move in a new direction with our artistic process. We discovered that we each had questions about how to explore unseen, unrecognized, and undervalued work historically done by women. Aware of our interests, Emily Rubin, a community arts and housing activist, invited us to create a performance for Loads of Prose, a DIY literary series located in neighborhood laundromats. People waited for their laundry to finish as they listened to a local poet or novelist, with a mic and portable amp, reading from their work. Rubin wondered how the two of us might create a new site-specific theater piece that could animate and deconstruct the stuff of laundry. Could dirty clothes, sheets, and towels become central to an investigation at the border of documentary and fiction, of being and re-enacting?

We accepted her proposal and decided that our focus would be on the people whose job it is to wash and fold a customer's "drop off" loads of laundry—weighing eight to forty pounds—in storefront businesses across New York City. Our field research began by trying to interview English-, Chinese-, and Spanish-speaking workers in New York City, but we soon discovered how reluctant our "informants" were to share thoughts about their jobs and their lives with the two of us, obvious outsiders. The questions we posed, as open and non-judgmental as they were intended to be, were often received as unwanted intrusions, exposing the structural problems built into a documentary paradigm involving explicit forms of interrogation.

We put away our recording devices but continued visiting laundromats, listening to people and writing notes on what we heard. Journalist Luo Xiaoyuan joined us in stores with Chinese speaking employees, enabling people to speak more freely in their own first language. Later, in the creation of our work together, we would expand upon this linguistic fissure by examining the sensation and frustration of not understanding what is being spoken.

Fortunately, some of the laundry workers we met did agree to become active participants in our project and were enthusiastic about being in front of the camera. Lulabelle Holloway, a thirty-year veteran of a commercial laundry center, and Wing Hung Ho, owner of his own storefront laundromat, appear in our documentary material and their verbatim interviews are an integral element of our playscript. Margarita Lopez, who supports her two sons through her work in a laundromat, offered her sharp observations to the performance projects and now to this book.

All of this source material initially coalesced into *Every Fold Matters*, a mixed media live performance about the work of doing laundry. Our first site-specific show happened on a frigid February night at New Lucky Laundromat in the Clinton Hill neighborhood of Brooklyn. Fifty people crowded in, sitting on top of machines and old folding chairs, our filmed segments coming out of a dusty TV hanging from the ceiling. From the start, we included film elements as part of the ontology of our theatrical environment. Our audience could be in the moment of the play but also recognize the simultaneity of other realities, with cinema fracturing both time and space.

After New Lucky laundromat, we moved our film/performance project to other non-traditional venues like the Amalgamated Lithographers Union Hall and the University Settlement House, and finally to The Tank, an alternative theater that embraces experimentation and accessibility. Audiences witnessed the seemingly mundane world of laundry through a personal and social lens, not as pure narrative but rather as an avant-garde adventure in hybrid spectatorship. *Every Fold Matters* asks how a person cares for the things worn closest to the body. Heightened dialogue and gestural, choreographed sequences, set amidst the washers and dryers of a laundromat, reveal stories of intimacy, dirt, stains, money, and time.

Dramatic interpretations of historical incidents also provide a critical element to our theatrical exploration. Our discovery of the Washing Society, a Reconstruction-era collective of Black women laundry workers who organized for higher pay in Atlanta, was crucial to our project. As a ghost figure from this brief radical moment in history, a member of the Washing Society emerges as a character in our play, suggesting a convergence of *what is* with an imagined *what was*. Primary source material, in the form of letters, manifestos, and newspaper accounts, provides this character with messages from the past that she delivers to the current day workers in the laundromat. We experience her otherworldly yet earth-bound presence. Embodied by actor Jasmine Holloway, she speaks with stature and ferocity, bringing to life the words and actions of a Black labor movement prior to the Jim Crow era of oppression and segregation. In her passionate address to the audience, she breaks the proverbial fourth wall.

We invited actors to devise the performance with us. They each drew from their own experiences doing laundry with their families and in work situations. The play's eponymous characters of Vera, Ching, Jasmine, and Tony were born from the identities of the actors themselves, confronting the dynamic between who they are in their lives and the dramatic roles they inhabit as workers and a customer in an imagined laundromat. Through an open and generative rehearsal process, we collectively developed the source material that we'd gathered, shaping it into scenes, monologues, and movement sequences. Props like rolling laundry carts, piles of quarters, and bottles of detergent became part of the vocabulary of this choreographic and textual construction.

The use of projected film images in our live performance repositions the body, altering scale and bringing the past into the present. In one scene, Ching dances in front of her projected film image, producing a silhouette of her body. In a close up, she tells the story of Tony, a customer who left $100 in the pocket of the pants that he's put into the wash. He instructs Ching to watch his load and leaves for several hours. She then finds the money and deliberates whether to return it. The reproduction of Ching on film is juxtaposed with her living, breathing body there in the room, in performance. The projected close-up of her head looms large, in contrast to the smallness of her full body in person. This inversion of scale produces a sense of disorientation acknowledging both the character's and our subjectivity.

In working with our verbatim interviews and conversations, we had to grapple with the impulse to translate from Chinese and Spanish to English for our audience; there are situations where we consciously resist this convention altogether. Our choice not to translate brings attention to the sound and texture of a person's "mother tongue" rather than privileging English. The acoustic beauty of these languages is then highlighted. In our calculated decision not to provide subtitles, we hope to challenge English as the global *lingua franca*.

We toured for two years with our performance *Every Fold Matters* yet still wanted to expand upon its themes, this time convinced that immersing ourselves in the making of a stand-alone film would give us the chance to expand our vision. We titled this film, the second iteration of our ongoing project, *The Washing Society*. Certain ideas could be more fully communicated through the vocabulary of the camera. Choosing to fill the frame with a person's hand or the reflection of sky in a storefront window provides its own layered story. A swirl of wet, colorful clothes spinning over and over and over reminds us of a cyclical tedium. A sequence of laundromat signs cuts to a single woman quietly contemplating a pile of clothes. Through sharply honed editing, we try to create visual tensions and transitions that reveal the omnipresent rhythms of a city filled with the machinery of cleaning.

Our cast and crew was composed of film and theater people, including a cinematographer, a sound artist, and an editor who became deeply involved in searching for new ways of looking at cleaning, laundry, and service work in the city where we all live or have lived. Cinematographer Sean Hanley used special magnification lenses to investigate the haunting, visceral qualities of lint. In the spirit of *musique concrète,* sound artist Stephen Vitiello built a multi-layered, percussive soundtrack out of the raw aural material from laundromats. Editor Amanda Katz immersed herself in the community of the laundromat on her block in Brooklyn. Walking the streets of New York City with our camera, the two of us collected observational footage that invited the viewer to contemplate the laundromat as an enclave.

Elements of our original performance *Every Fold Matters* are integrated into *The Washing Society* but as heightened, intentional moments dancing at the edge of naturalism. Real laundromat workers appear in long takes and close ups, sometimes speaking directly to the camera. The ambiguity of hybrid filmmaking itself manifests when we see these verité images of laundry workers juxtaposed with actors performing. Our film premiered at the Carter G. Woodson Institute of African American Studies in Richmond, Virginia, and then traveled to venues around the country including the Brooklyn Academy of Music's CinemaFest, Berkeley's Pacific Film Archive, Washington, DC's National Gallery of Art, Memphis's National Civil

Rights Museum, and internationally to Bosnia, Ecuador, England, Ireland, and Spain.

Hand Book: A Manual on Performance, Process, and the Labor of Laundry marks our third iteration. Here, we construct a space for readers to think about the politics and history of service work, art-making, and aesthetic experimentation. The book aims to provide an evolving model for a collaborative, socially engaged practice, one that emerges from a system of relationships both in front of and behind the curtain and the camera. Our playscript gives readers the opportunity to enter the world we created. Read this text as you would a recipe or a set of instructions for an event that you are being invited to make happen in your head. For us, this playscript forms the backbone of our entire project and is the core of *Hand Book: A Manual*.

Readers will also find reflections by our performers in the book. During our rehearsals, they would shape, stuff, roll, throw, stretch, and hide within familiar pieces of clothing transforming them into sculptural abstractions. The machines and furniture of the laundromat also prompted intense physical responses, like the iconic folding table as a place for improvisation. Dancer and actor Veraalba Santa writes about developing her personal and highly physical dance composition erupting from the folding of invisible clothes. Actor Jasmine Holloway recounts discovering that her grandmother worked in a commercial laundry for thirty years. She also uses her character's historical costume as a member of the Washing Society to reflect on her own Black female identity.

Never a neutral endeavor, the writing of history transforms evidence, potentially making what was invisible more visible. Throughout our process, we connected our source material to a larger story, specifically the activities of the Washing Society as a singular moment in American history when a group of Black washerwomen came together in 1881 to demand higher wages for their work. Historian and author Tera Hunter became a part of our project early on when we were introduced to her highly-influential book *To 'Joy My Freedom: Southern Black Women's Lives and Labors after the Civil War*. We spoke with Hunter about her uncovering of this story of Black, female resistance and her thoughts about our theatrical interpretation. Her research led us to a series of archival pages from Atlanta's major newspaper at the time. By including them in our book, we give readers a vivid sense of the historical context of the washerwomen's remarkable strike. These journalistic artifacts of clearly biased reporting from a Post-Civil War South publication helped us to imagine the group's struggle for autonomy, a critical thread in our play. Adding to this perspective, labor historian Andrea Estepa reminds us of the way service work can be a gloss for servitude.

The writing of feminist historian and activist Silvia Federici, author of *Caliban and the Witch* and one of the founders of the Wages for Housework movement in the 1970s, has been vital to us. We were deeply influenced by her consideration of women's work in the home which she defines as *reproductive labor* with its own distinct yet unrecognized social and economic value under capitalism.

We wrote a letter to Federici to see if she would be willing to meet and speak with us. We invited her to take a walk in Brooklyn's Prospect Park where we discussed her theory of reproductive labor in relation to laundry work. Later, we visited her apartment where we continued to talk about the role of essential workers, particularly during the recent years of the global pandemic. This initial meeting turned into a friendship which grew in ways we never would have expected. As we continued our work on *Hand Book*, our visits with Federici have given us the opportunity to think more fully about the body in space, the shared resources of the *commons*, and art as a form of resistance. It is moving to both of us to see that Silvia's work is having an impact on the next generation of feminists who see the interrelationship between our economic system, the oppression of women and immigrants.

Looking toward the potential for engagement in all forms of art-making, we include the voices of members of the Laundry Workers Center, a vibrant, dedicated group of grassroots labor organizers who work to educate and support the collective actions of laundry workers in New York City. We came to know two leaders from this organization, Mahoma López and Rosanna Rodríguez, who spoke at several of our film presentations. In our book, they share their immigration stories and their evolution as activists.

Hand Book: A Manual conveys our journey as artists through performance documentation, film stills, and a vital series of photographs we call "In Motion." As co-authors, we enter into a dialogue that exposes the vulnerability of making work that might not say what we thought it would, work that might fail to fulfill its fundamental intentions. Toward the end of *Hand Book*, we talk about a singular historic photo by Gertrude Kasbier, a nineteenth-century woman photographer whose white gaze mirrors ours and shakes us into a form of reckoning with our own identity. In two diaristic pieces, each of us reveals our doubts related to family and care. Our book is a question, asking what it means to witness, compose, and represent the experiences of others as filtered through our own subjectivity.

Throughout our process, we think about the intimacy of touching other people's clothes, almost like a second skin—tending to things kept close to the body. The relationship between a laundry worker and a customer, a home care attendant to a patient, a manicurist with a client, can be fraught and complex. Our multi-year engagement with participants in this project confirms the precarious reality of all of these service industries. In our performance, film, and now this book, we re-play these convergences as aspects of the social contract that structures city life.

You are the audience now,
reading a book instead of watching and listening,
turning the page,
moving from one discourse to another,
holding a container,
its contours informed by our thoughts,
and in turn,
shaping your experience.

—Lizzie Olesker and Lynne Sachs

INTRODUCTION

Chan Laundromat
Happy Laundromat
Chee & Yun Laundromat
Kang Wei Laundromat
Evergreen Laundromat
Sun & Moon Laundromat
Lams Laundromat
Goody Laundromat & Dry Cleaners
Zheng Laundromat
Nice Laundromat & Dry Clean
New Lucky Laundromat
Super Suds Laundromat
Gentle Wash Laundromat

A Thousand Pieces a Day

*Margarita Lopez (laundromat worker,
speaking directly to the camera in the film* The Washing Society)

Well, I'm using my hands as soon as I get into work. I'm putting laundry into the washer, using my hands to put in the quarters. Then, when it's finished, I have to stand there and fold. Fold however many pounds. It could be as little as one pound to 100 pounds and it may take me fifteen minutes or it may take me an hour and a half so I'm doing the same motion over and over again.

When we're finished and we're stacked up and we have our bags, we have to lift those bags and we're lifting twenty, thirty, forty, fifty pounds. So now I have a herniated disc which I didn't have before working here.

I've found cellphones. I've found money. You find drugs. You find needles. You find… razors, wallets, licenses, IDs…. You never know what you're going to find.

You have people that treat you like human beings, and you have people that treat you in a certain way, just because you work in a laundromat, you're just, I don't know, lesser than them or whatever the case may be, whatever they feel.

And you know you get a lot of racism, I feel racism. Not only because I'm a Latina, but just because I am working in a laundromat. So, they'll just come and they'll throw stuff at you. They'll be like: Here, I want this done and that's it. Like, not even a hello, not even a good morning. Their tone of voice is very negative and it's just, you know….

That particular person that day, I was like: good morning, how are you? And, you know, he was just very nasty to me. He was very nasty and, um, he didn't want to deal with me because I was, I guess, Spanish.

You know, there were a lot of people in the laundromat. He used the words that he decided to use, and the things that he decided to say. They were uncalled for. All I was doing was my job, asking him his phone number, asking him what he wanted, if he wanted separation or no separation. He just didn't want to deal with me at all.

He called me a couple of names and I was just, like, you know, I'm not dealing with you. My boss comes, he can deal with you. I'm not doing your clothes. And he said, uh, that I was going to get fired, uh, that I didn't have any papers and I was like, okay, whatever. Yeah, he was like, you don't have no papers, that's why you're working here. And I'm like, *unbelievable*.

On a normal day, on a normal nine-hour day, I do myself—I'm not saying they're all heavy—but I do no less than twenty-five to twenty-six bags a day. I think that I fold over 1,000 pieces of clothes a day. And... you know, just little articles, socks, you know, underwear. All of them have to be turned inside-out, one by one. Every piece counts.

If I had to say... I would say, I fold 1,000 pieces a day or more. A week... it would probably be... I'm working four times a week at this moment, so it's, it'll be, like, 4,000 pieces a week, so in a month it would be over 12,000 pieces. And that's just what I think, it could be more. I know it can't be less, I know it's more.

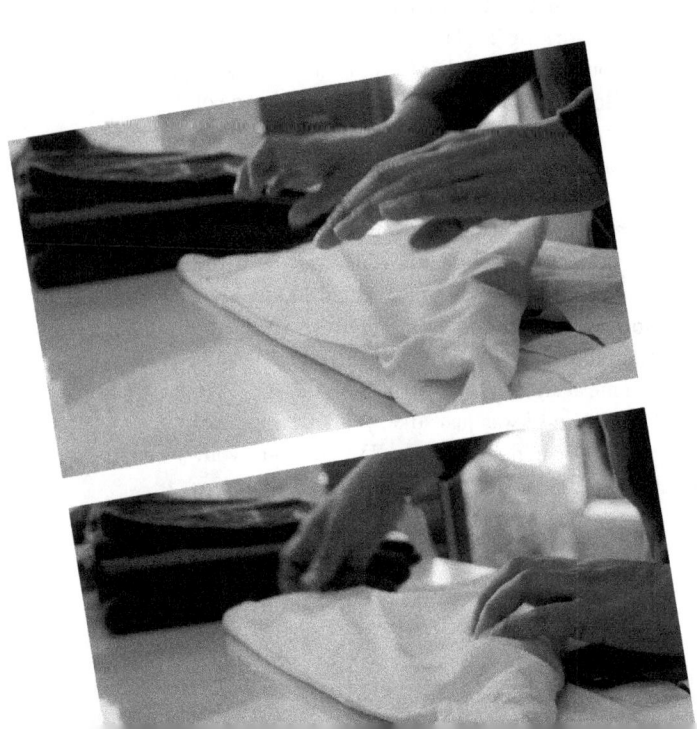

LINT

Lynne Sachs

Inside the machine
inverted colossal bags of upside-down families
children spin with bedridden grandparents
dog-mats hug the underside of workout pants
party blouses rub elbows with gardening jeans
aprons with chicken grease from bitter family fight
keys left in pockets
subway cards worth $45 (or maybe not)
underwear stained vaguely pink inside the sleeve of
blue striped button-down shirt
withered gym shorts nestled against a single sock
unwanted thread.
Salvage a twisted $50 bill so you can pay for a dinner
that ends up on a t-shirt under a fleece jacket
made from old tires and recycled plastic.
Fleece is not real,
who knew?

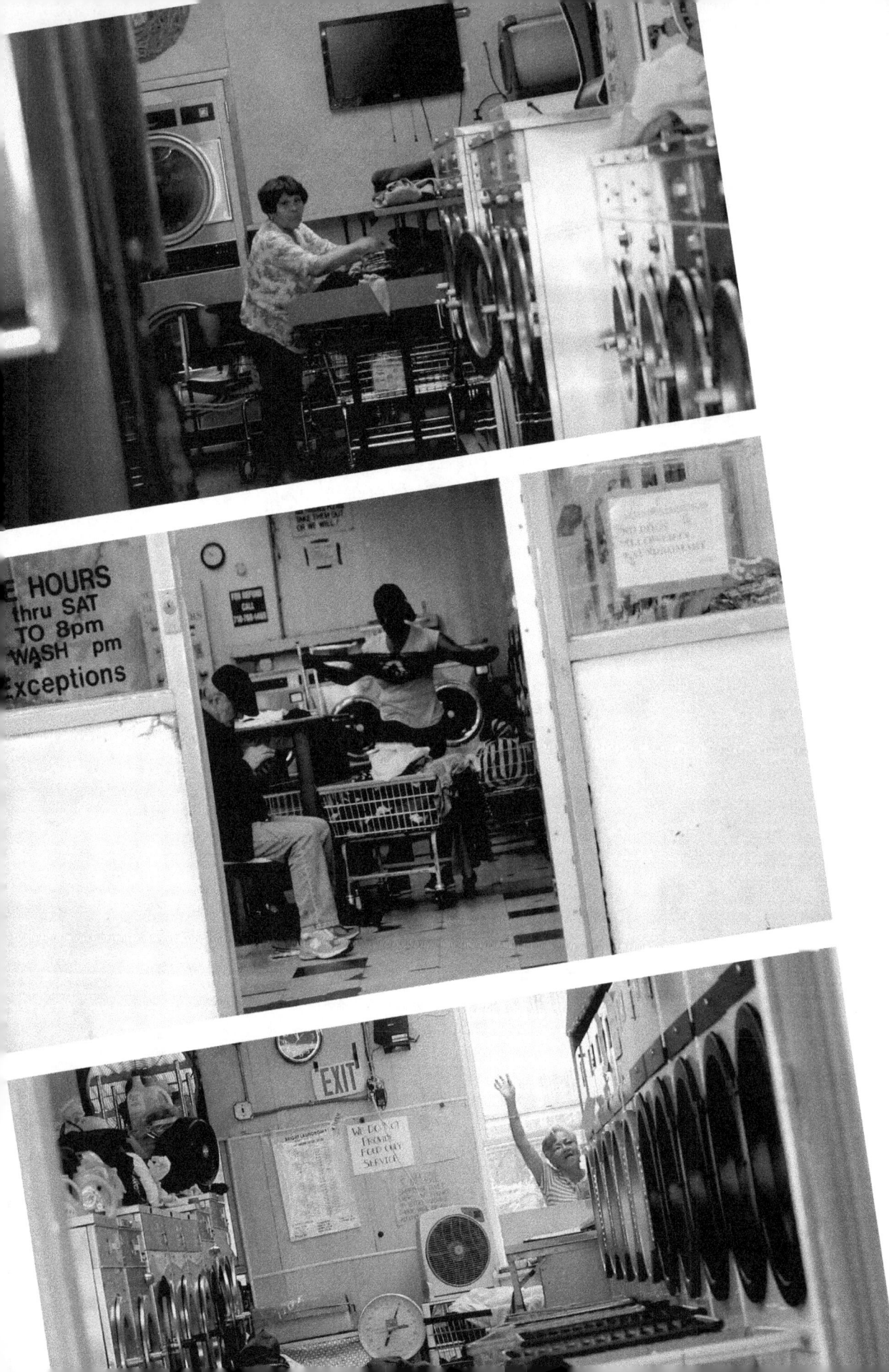

FINDING THE STAIN: A TRANSCRIPT IN TRANSLATION

interviews and translations by Luo Xiaoyua

Interviewee #1: Mr. Ho (何), 299 Broome Street, Tai Loong Laundromat

How long have you worked here?
I've been working here for twenty years, but I'm not the owner.

Do customers hide the stains?
No, they never hide stains. In fact, they will point them out, and ask me for help to clean the dirty spots.

Do you bring your own laundry?
I bring my clothes to the place I work. Doing laundry at home is a waste of time. You have to wash, then hang dry and then clean up. But if you bring them here, it just takes an hour or so.

How have your customers changed?
Before, our customers were all Chinese, but rentals in this neighborhood are going up day by day, and some Chinese residents who can't afford the housing moved out, while people from other races came in. So, right now we have much more diverse customer backgrounds. Also, people preferred to use drop-off service in the past, but now they are more likely to use self-service while killing the time by playing on their smartphones.

Can you describe your job?
Only by loving your job, can you do the best. Therefore, loving whatever you are doing is a must. Another thing is my working shift. It is too long, literally from 6:00 AM to 8:00 PM. I feel sorry for my family and kids as I rarely have time to accompany them. When people are enjoying holidays, we have to work.

What if people leave money in their clothes?
Most of the time, we will hold the money and return it to the customers. I remember it was the eve before Chinese New Year, our laundromats were full of people washing their clothes. One customer who used the dryer left $1,500 in his pocket. Since it was extremely busy, lots of customers used that dryer. When he came back, there was no trace of his money and I swore I'd seen nothing. But he insisted that it was me who stole the money. People also forget their clothes. Some will come back to pick up after leaving their clothes in here for more than six months. Others even forgot to pick up after one or two years.

Can you describe an unusual moment?
Last week, one customer's clothes' color changed a little bit. I informed them of the problem, but they weren't listening. For some, missing clothes makes them angry. But for others, missing clothes is not a big deal.

Interviewee #2: Chris, 48 Mulberry Street, TLC Dry Cleaners Inc.

Do you recognize people by their clothes?
I could tell people's jobs from the clothes they are wearing, like a policeman's uniform. Expensive shirts imply a decent job.

Tell us about some unusual things that have happened here.
Some customers might try to scam me. They sometimes hide the stains on their clothes, or put the dirtiest clothes at the bottom of other clothes. Because they're worrying if I find the stains (which are usually hard to get rid of), then I won't take their clothes. Another guy even complained he lost one of his pieces of clothing just to scam me to pay the money. One customer parked his car outside and came in to drop off his clothes. Unfortunately, he got a ticket. And he was angry at me because he thought it was my fault to make him get the ticket, complaining I was working too slow.

Where are you from?
I'm from Hong Kong. There are no laundromats in Hong Kong. Nobody does your laundry for you. Everyone has a washing machine at home. People will just hang the clothes until they dry. In my family—my mother is a housewife—she has plenty of time to wash the clothes, hang dry, and sometimes iron the shirts. Back there, I helped my mother with the easiest stuff, like folding underwear.

Interviewee #3: Young Woman, 28 Orchard Street, Orchard Cleaners & Laundromat

How long have you worked here?
I've been working at the laundromat for three years. We are usually extremely busy on Mondays and Wednesdays, while Sundays are very quiet.

Can you tell us about the service?

We've been running this business for decades. Our customers are more than acquaintances. We know each other. They often drop off their clothes before they go to work.

Can you use five words to describe your job?
Tired but happy.

What is the best and worst part about your work?
Most of the customers are nice, only one was picky. He complained about the stains left on his clothes, saying, "You guys are cleaners, you should take care of this." We then washed the clothes for him again with no charge, but still cannot get rid of the deep stains. He yelled at us and didn't foot the bill. But he would come back again to use our service and do his laundry.
   I have no extra time to focus on my own stuff.

Can you describe an unusual moment?
Many customers leave their Kindles, iPhones, or other tablets in their pockets. We usually hold the devices for them. It goes the same with the money. Even if there is just $1 in their pocket, we will save it for the customers. But if they're just pennies, we'll just keep it for ourselves.

Interviewee #4: Woman, 35 Allen Street, Grandma Laundromat

Do you do a lot of folding?
I learned folding when I was working in another laundromat nearby. In the beginning, I had no idea how to do it. But once you saw others fold, then you practiced and made your own improvements.

What is the best and worst part about your work?
Nothing is bad. I'm just part-time, so it's fine. The best part is to meet different people and chat with them.... Are you from the government?

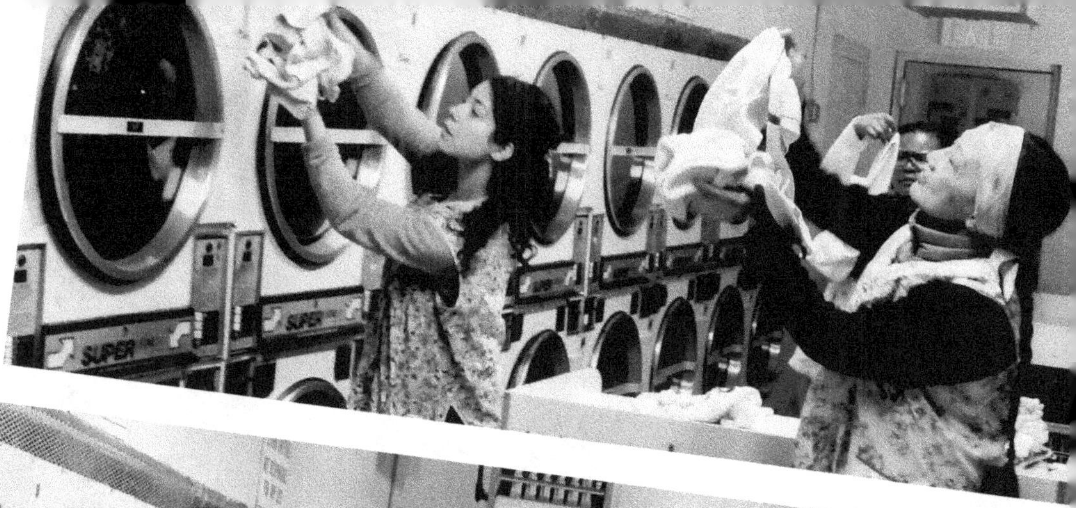
SUPER

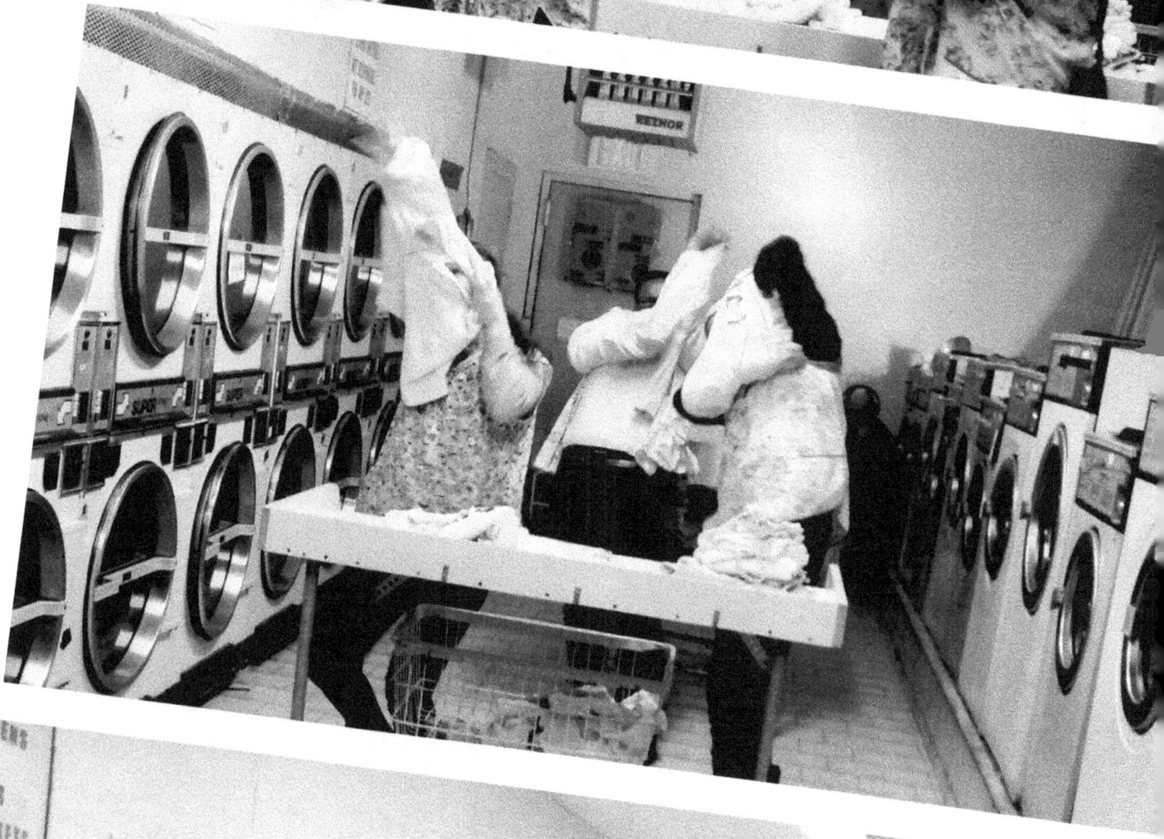
SUPER

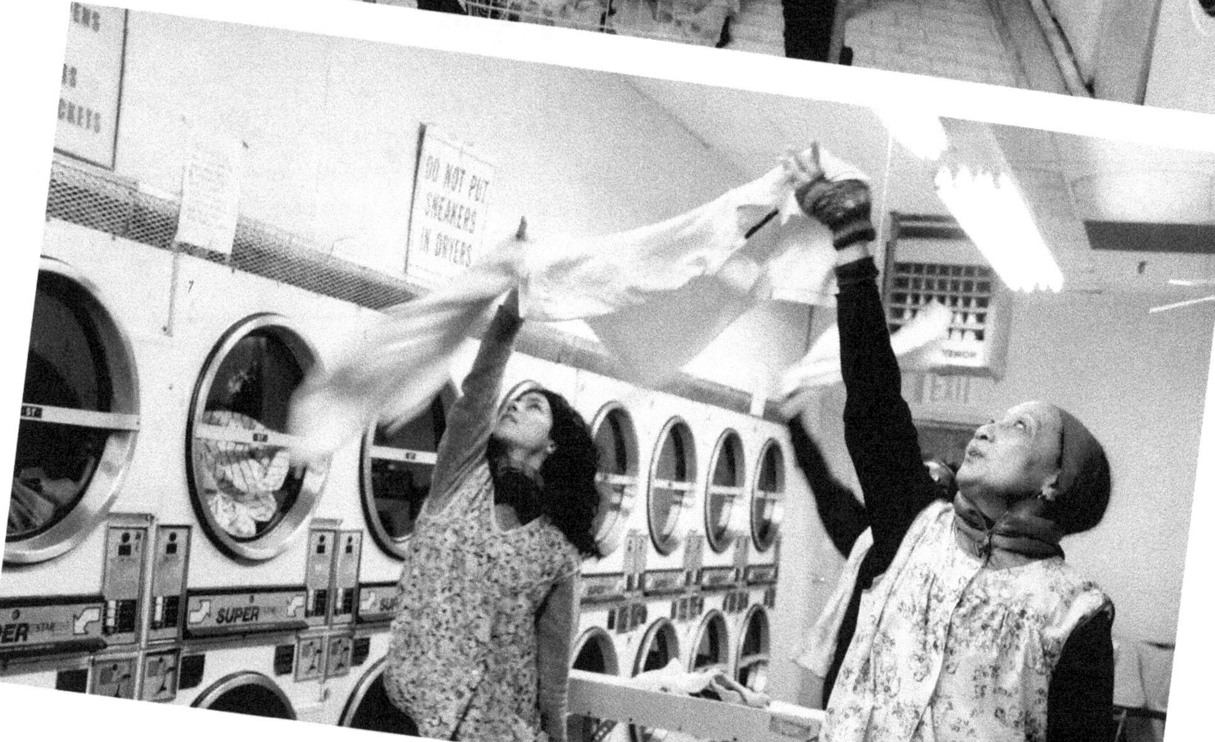
DO NOT PUT SNEAKERS IN DRYERS
SUPER

score for a folding dance

composed and performed by Veraalba Santa

— Stand still at the table. Pull imagined fabric with both hands from left to center.
— Lay "fabric" at center of table. Fold again towards the center-right section of the table.
— Work your way down and up with fingers as if buttoning a shirt in rapid motion.
— Fold from right to left while gaze is facing the right side of the room (*bored? looking out the window? or at the clock? lunch break? is this shift almost over?*).
— Flap, flip, and fold aimlessly. Fold up once towards the left side of the table.
— Spin away. Land on the right side of the table and fold again with floppy forearms.
— Leaning over the table, you flip hands over twice at the same time. Shake large "fabric" and let it float across the table.
— Pause. Tap foot repeatedly looking towards the right side of the table again (*clock? client? boss?*). Tap fingers repeatedly on the table, still looking towards the right side.
— Shake "fabric" and let it float down.
— Looking in various directions, fold repeatedly towards the right side of the table (*looking at clients? checking the machines?*).
— Hands hitting the table, getting louder with each fold. Make a small fold on right side of table. Reach one arm towards the left side. Pull inward towards the right side of the table.
— Hold. Fold "fabric" into a square. Repeat floppy forearm fold.
— Slam both hands on table four times with a slight swoosh. Right arm rises as if about to spin—(*but decide not to*).
— Rhythm changes. Pat table. BaDabaDabaDabah. Pick up corners and fold quickly.
— Wrists loosely fold. Wipe lint off clothing and arms.
— Repeat—Look in various directions four times with more urgency.
— Torso and shoulders become more involved with folding (*becoming the fabric, the table, the task*). Heavier energy.

— Small folding gesture with hands. Flip hands three times towards the left side of table.
— Large blanket floats over the table. Stretch "fabric" three times; fold downwards and look away.
— Flip, flap, pick lint and flick it away. Start folding again.

The body spins over the table as if it is folding itself or embodying tumbling clothes being thrown from a hamper basket. Internal sensations involving elements of exhaustion, routine, and time are discovered. Intersperse physical gestures like scratching and removing lint from a sleeve. The sequence evolves. Everything becomes a part of the dance: the sound and smell of the quarters, the metal, the doors slamming. The body is climbing, sweating, folding, and slamming across the machines as if becoming one. And then back to folding.

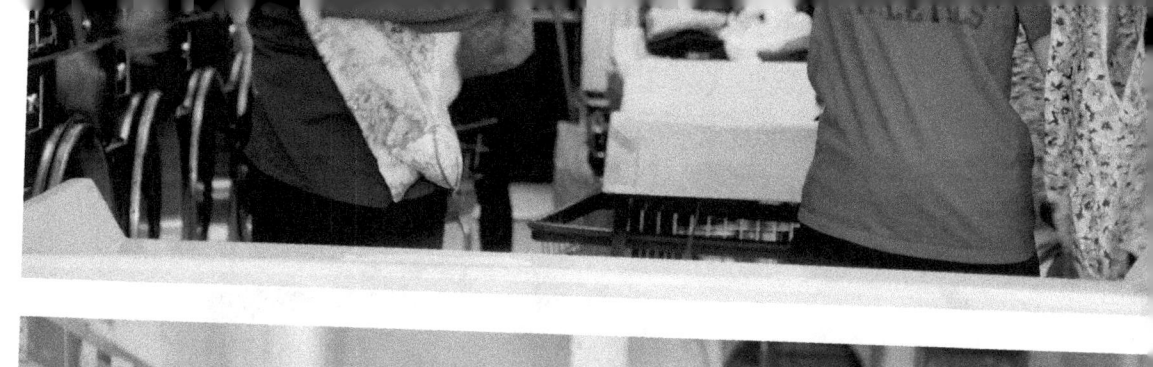

Every Fold Matters

a playscript

by Lizzie Olesker and Lynne Sachs

The women of the Washing Society used the practical skills they had learned in grassroots politics. Their spirited rallies with prayers, speeches, and singing in black churches closely resembled the form of other political meetings. The period from 1879 to 1881 was a brief time of opportunity, and African-Americans pressed it as far as they could before the full force of New South political and economic development made itself felt.
— Tera Hunter, *To 'Joy My Freedom: Southern Black Women's Lives and Labors After the Civil War*

CHARACTERS

CHING (60s)	Filipina laundromat worker
VERAALBA (30s)	Latina laundromat worker
JASMINE (20s)	African-American woman laundromat worker
	Ghost Figure, a member of the Washing Society of 1881
TONY (50s)	White male customer who does his own laundry
	Upscale Drop-Off Customer

REAL PEOPLE ON SCREEN

WING HUNG HO	Laundromat worker and owner, Chinatown
LULA HOLLOWAY	Retired laundry worker, Upper West Side

NOTES

Filmed segments are interwoven into the live performance. They come out of the laundromat's TV, or are projected onto a wall or a sheet.

Gestural choreography and staging can be developed in relation to spatial elements of a working laundromat where live performances take place.

There should be two laundry carts, a large table for folding, and several chairs.

We see many loads of laundry (clothes, sheets, pillowcases, etc.) in piles, baskets, and bags, waiting to be washed and folded. Some of the clothes have single words printed on them.

Other props include clothespins, clothesline, and pairs of red-palmed workers' gloves. There are also doll-sized clothes that appear during the performance.

Margin Notes provide context for the research involved in the writing of the play.

Actors Ching Valdes-Aran, Veralba Santa, Jasmine Holloway, and Tony Torn helped devise and perform the original production of *Every Fold Matters* (2015-2018).

As the audience enters, each person
receives a small piece of lint to
hold in their hand.

   Inside a Brooklyn neighborhood
   laundromat. Dusty windows protect
   the cramped space filled with machines and dryers on a weathered
   linoleum floor.

   In a corner of the laundromat, hud-
   dled against a warm dryer, Tony, a
   customer, sits restlessly waiting
   for his load to finish.

   A woman in full nineteenth-century
   dress is sitting in a chair, in
   profile. Perfectly still and silent, she appears to be from another time, the Ghost Figure.

The laundromat's machines spin, the dryers hum, and the
smell of detergent permeates the air.

Ching and Vera appear — they work here. They speak directly to us, their lines overlapping.

Note: Lint is a combination of many things, including clothing remnants, plant fiber, hair, dead skin cells, and dust. A form of residue left after a wet garment is dried in a machine, lint usually accumulates as a form of detritus we are trained to throw away as quickly and efficiently as possible. By sharing these tangible substances with our audience, we are making a gesture that challenges the abject qualities of waste and dirt. Perhaps a member of the audience will throw this souvenir on the floor, perhaps they will play with it for a while. Either way, we are asking them to think about lint and its association with touching another person's body.

CHING
I don't want to talk about it.

VERA
Nothing to /
sorry.

CHING
Let's talk about something else / not today.

VERA
Don't want to say /
sorry.

CHING
Nothing / sorry.

VERA
Why do you want to know?

CHING
Nothing interesting.

VERA
Just a job.

CHING
My boss says no.

> *The sounds of water transform into music. Vera and Ching push and pull their laundry carts across the floor in a pattern, weaving in and out, spinning around each other. They take clothes from the carts, picking up speed. Words are written on each piece — a child's dress with the word POCKET, a pair of women's underwear with the word BUTTON, a man's dress shirt with the word DRAIN — and, depending on where they are in relation to each other, these words become short poetic phrases. The women hold up different pieces of clothing, look at the word combinations they've created, playfully displaying and discarding them. Then moving on to the next words, and the next:*

time	pocket
fold	button
zip	stain
me	deep
hole	zipper
mouth	tug
drain	stain
inside	she

The Ghost Figure speaks.

Note: How would a nineteenth-century washerwoman describe the work that she does? We wondered where to find an accurate description of the process of taking in laundry.

Where do we go to find this information? However incongruous, we resort to the internet and google things like: "pre-industrial laundry soap" and "washtub materials."

GHOST FIGURE
I take in laundry just like so many, earning four to eight dollars a month, more hours than I can count. I have increased my earnings of late with the adding on of several new clients and the help of my children. Like you, I take in loads on Monday mornings, returning the clean goods on Saturday. Our soap is made from lye, starch, and wheat bran, and we make our washtubs from beer barrels cut in half. We carry our water from the well. Pump and hydrate down the road, boiling and rinsing and hanging in our own homes. We press using a few

hot irons at a time and weather permitting, we work outside, too, in the shade.

Ching moves her arms in flowing circular gestures as Vera's shoulders, hands, and face twitch; together, they create a dance.

CHING
I think about other things when I'm doing it.

My mind wanders.

VERA
All you get is their name and their bag of dirty stuff. You write it on a tag, a tag for all that sweat, coffee, period stains, and... whatever.

CHING
You know nothing about them, but you also know more than you want to know, you know?

VERA
It's a personal thing, if you think about it.

It's like getting to open up someone else's closet, someone you don't know. Seeing what's inside. You can tell someone's story just by what they've worn, how it's dirty, you know?

CHING
My mother —

She showed me.

I used to —

No dryers. Just hang dry.
I helped my mother with the easiest stuff. Like, folding underwear.

And then you practice, practice, practice.

VERA
Make your own improvements.

I do it like this. Fold one, two, three.

See? My way.

CHING
I work part-time, six- or seven-hour shifts, five-to-six days a week.

VERA
I meet different people.

I almost remember each face. Almost... each face of every customer.

> Tony, the customer, returns to the laundromat carrying a paper bag with a to-go cup of coffee and a greasy sandwich. He starts to pull his clothes from the dryer, realizing that someone has already removed them and put them in a laundry cart. He picks up a shirt to see if it's dry. It's not — everything's still damp. He glares at the dryer, looking at someone else's load spinning there. He angrily bangs on the dryer door, and turns to the person sitting closest to the machine, the Ghost Figure.

TONY
Hey, is this yours?

Is this your stuff? Because that was my stuff in the dryer and you took it out. You touched my clothes.

Can't you see they weren't done?

So, you just opened the door, took out my stuff, and dumped it here in the cart, didn't you? It's still wet. Here, you feel that? You feel that?! They're still wet. You must have touched my clothes. Couldn't you feel that they're still wet? Let's see how you like it —

> Tony opens the dryer door mid-cycle, pulls out a damp shirt and aggressively throws it at her.

TONY
WHAT DO YOU THINK? THIS DRYER BELONGS TO YOU?

> Tony storms out of the laundromat, carrying his wet clothes in his arms.
> The Ghost Figure disappears.

> A shift.

> Jasmine enters and puts on a flowered smock. It's the first day of her new job in this laundromat.

She awkwardly approaches her new co-workers, Vera and Ching, who are busy pulling loads from the dryers, placing them into carts. All three women move to a large table at the center of the laundromat, and begin to fold, fold, fold.

Note: The table provides an anchor. It is the place the characters continually return to, repeatedly folding. It is also another kind of stage on which hands and bodies perform. Smaller and more contained, the table's surface becomes a microcosm. By playing with scale, our perception of reality expands and contracts.

VERA
What's happening with machine number 12? You got that?

CHING
Yah, yah. I got it, I got it.

JASMINE
Uh... where should I put my stuff?

CHING
Right here under the counter.

VERA
Don't worry, no one is going to bother it.

JASMINE
You want me to — ?

CHING
You sit there. You watch.

JASMINE
You sure you don't want me —

VERA
You got number 12 or not? There's something that smells like shit in there.

JASMINE
The other place I worked at, they made us wear gloves all the time.

VERA
What's for lunch today?

CHING
What do you think?

VERA
Heads you buy, tails you lose.

CHING
Ha — you wish, lady.

JASMINE
I got turkey on a roll.

I don't need the whole thing — you can have half.

CHING
No thank you.

VERA *(referring to Tony, reentering)*
Here he comes, again.

CHING
And again.

VERA
He comes in all the time — you'll see. He sits here with his paper —

CHING
His bologna sandwich —

JASMINE
Oh no!

VERA
He just parks himself right here.

CHING
All day, sometimes.

VERA
It's like, hello — don't you have anywhere else to go, mister?

TONY *(to the audience)*
A roll of quarters, a cup of coffee to go, a newspaper. Sometimes the ladies talk to me. Sometimes they don't.

CHING
I'm getting 22 into the dryer. They'll come to pick up soon.

VERA
Here's ticket number 63 from the restaurant.

JASMINE *(to herself)*
Everyone needs a place to go.

CHING
Hand me that bag. That one, with the stripes.

JASMINE *(eager to help)*
You got it.

   Tony holds up a pair of boxer shorts.

TONY *(to audience)*
How do you know it's time to do it?

You don't have any clean underwear, bottom line.

You can get away with socks but not dirty underwear. Besides, it's very cold out there, warm in here.

   Tony quietly retreats to his favorite spot behind the machines, only partially visible, to change his clothes. We realize that he needs to come here, to this public laundromat, as a place to stay warm, hang out, and clean himself up.

CHING *(in a reverie, almost to herself)*
There are all kinds, growing.

Rows and rows of dahlias… also, jackfruit, chili peppers, and okra. Back home…

VERA
You know that lady, the one who always brings her organic detergent when she drops off?

CHING
They're all around my yard, my door, by the window. My favorites are the yellow ones, so happy looking. They make everyone feel happy.

VERA
Yeah, so the other day, she hands me the detergent and she says it again, the same

- 7 -

thing, like she does every time she drops her stuff off, like I forgot or I'm stupid or something.

CHING
And when the sun is out — oh my! Those flowers look gorgeous.

VERA
She goes, this is very important. Listen! I'm allergic to your soap — the smell. A-ller-gic: *comprendez?* Yeah, I understand, I say back to her. I break out in a rash, she says. I know, I say, I know. I do, too. Little red bumps on my arms, my hands —

JASMINE
I bet those flowers back home smell good, right?

CHING
I don't know —

VERA
But the lady's not even listening. She's on her cell. She snaps her fingers like this (snaps) so I can give her the ticket.

CHING
They send me pictures. That's it.

VERA
So, I do her stuff and a bunch of other bags. We were busy.

CHING
Every single day. When they bloom, when they die, my garden.

JASMINE
Wow. And the kids, your grandkids — ?

CHING
Oh yeah, everybody. I see everything. They make sure to text and send me pictures.

VERA
And I suddenly think, maybe I forgot, maybe I didn't use her detergent, her stupid fucking organic shit, but if I tell her, she'll be so pissed and tell the boss, or she could post some shit on us. But if I don't tell her, then she might really break out in a bad rash and it would be my fault. (pause) My fault...

JASMINE
... Right?

VERA
But when she comes back to pick up, she's still on her cell and just hands me the ticket, with the money rolled up inside. When I give her back her clean stuff, she goes "gracias, keep the change," which was only two quarters — fifty cents! And I shove the coins in my jeans. (pause) And I can feel tiny red bumps coming up on my arms, on the palm of each hand, on my back —

CHING (responding to Vera)
That happened to my son once. He had those bumps.
I used to bring him to work with me here, when he was a kid.

VERA
The pain and itch coming up...

CHING
I had to take him to the ER.

VERA
Like maybe I'm being punished, or something.

CHING
I told the boss I had to take him, be with him, and he said, you expect me to believe that? Get your ass in here, get your ass in here!

VERA
He's the ass —

CHING
So I had no choice —
I got my friend to take him. My boy.
I was afraid the boss might fire me.
And at the end of the day, he comes up real close, puts a folded
$10 bill in my pocket, like I was one of those women who takes money for... you know...
$10 for doing what he told me to do.
I wanted to spit in his face —
But I didn't.

Tony puts on a suit jacket, and becomes the upscale Drop-Off Customer.

DROP-OFF CUSTOMER
I am here to pick up my laundry.

CHING
Where is your ticket?

He takes things from his pockets, looking desperately for his laundry ticket.

DROP-OFF CUSTOMER
I am so sorry. I forgot my ticket. I know I have it somewhere. Hold on. Let me check. Could you just look me up?

CHING
This is the last time. You always lose it.
(to Jasmine) Typical.

DROP-OFF CUSTOMER
Sorry, sorry. Thank you. Thank you... sorry... thanks... sorry, sorry...

Drop-off Customer leaves.
Ching and Vera begin to shimmy and shake, dancing as they speak confidentially to Jasmine.

VERA
Sometimes they get angry when they think the color changed —

CHING
Or a stain didn't come out.

VERA
They'll put the dirtiest clothes at the bottom of the other clothes. Use bleach, they say. Why are they so scared of a stain?

CHING
I've been in the laundry business longer than both of you have been alive. I know how to rescue a shirt. My customers count on me. They think I do magic.

Ching and Vera step away, leaving Jasmine alone.

JASMINE *(closing her eyes)*
I just want to stand in a shower and feel all the warm water pour down.
Not hot, we get enough hot here.
I would let it pour down my face and into my nose, my mouth... down my throat, washing away all the crud in my chest.
You walk into the laundry and you think it feels good, that clean smell and all.
But sometimes, those so-called good, "clean" things are not always so good for you, you know?

Shift.

Ching, Vera, and Jasmine are folding a pile of t-shirts.

The amplified sound of rhythmic breathing — building in layers — becomes an accompaniment to a series of synchronized, gestural work movements and then a dance, the T-Shirt Dance.

All three performers roll up a t-shirt, put it between their legs, and let it drop to the floor. Then they each pick up the shirt, swinging it like a lasso, high above their heads. Momentum builds. Scrunching it up into a tight ball, they hold it close to their chests. Leaning back, the women let their t-shirts fall, covering their faces.

The dance ends. Ching and Vera climb on top of the folding table and sit, back to back, sleeping.

Jasmine turns on the laundromat's TV.

A documentary film segment comes on the TV. This is an interview with Wing Hung Ho, laundromat worker.

MR. HO *(speaking in Chinese, with subtitles)*
$12.90. Thank you. Thank you. I've been working in the laundromat for sixteen years. I was an electric repairman before I came here, but the electronics factory moved to another state. In order to make a living, I had no choice but to come here. This laundromat belonged to my mother-in-law, but I took it over and began working here. My first child was born at that time. And I had to earn a living. During my sixteen years here, I've witnessed a lot of change in this neighborhood. In the beginning, Broome Street was really quiet. Now it's changed a lot. Many Chinese

immigrants have moved out of here and other races have moved in. Just like our drop-off service — we have more drop-offs than ever before. In the past, people typically washed their own clothes. Living in this neighborhood has become more expensive.

I'm done with my work after 7:00PM. We close at seven o'clock. My sons wait for me and we go home together. We head out for work every day at 7:00AM and work until 7:30PM. When we get home, it's already 8:00PM. Our daily life is quite routine. Go out early. Come back late.

Documentary film segment ends, and Jasmine turns off the TV.

Ching and Vera are now joined by Jasmine and all speak, their lines overlapping.

CHING *(in Tagalog)*
I don't want to talk about it.

VERA *(in Spanish)*
Nothing to say.

JASMINE *(in English)*
Let's talk about something else.

CHING
Not today.

Don't want to say — sorry.

JASMINE
Nothing — sorry.

CHING
Why do you want to know?

VERA
Nothing interesting — just a job.

CHING
The boss says no.

VERA
Sometimes the boss comes and watches you and he says, "Go faster, do more... come on, come on...."
This one time, a lady came in and she said I had ruined, RUINED, her favorite pants.
She said I'd broken the damn zipper and made a tear or some shit.
And I didn't even remember her stupid fucking pants.
So I go, "What pants, where?"
And she starts pointing her fingers at me and she goes, "You're gonna pay for it.
You're gonna pay for a new pair." She goes, "Those pants cost me eighty-five dollars," or some shit.
"I'm gonna talk to your boss, talk to the owner."
"Go ahead," I say.
And she says, "I'll make sure they take eighty-five dollars from your pay.
I'll make sure you pay for it, you little whore, you little bitch" —
I start to get mad now but I don't want to go off on her or anything, like I can sometimes.
So I just say, "Okay, show me the pants — the zipper."
So she opens up her bag — it's this big old plastic shopping bag — and it's filled with all kinds of shit like old magazines, wrappers, socks and pieces of food —
layers and layers of, like, garbage, you know?
So, now I see that something's not right with this lady. Something's all wrong. There were never any pants, no zipper, no rip.
At least, I don't think so.
She must've been looking for something else from me.

Ching and Vera take both elegant and awkward poses, creating laundry "sculptures and attitudes" with clothes.

Vera picks up a polyester print shirt from the cart and pulls it over her head and face. Ching hides her head inside a sleeve.

CHING
I don't look at what customers are putting in, what they're folding.
I don't look at their clothes, but sometimes you can't help it, you know? Sometimes they hide the

Note: In his short story "Fin del juego" ("End of the Game"), Argentine-French author Julio Cortázar describes four early-adolescent girls performing "sculptures and attitudes" for commuters passing by on a train who become their anonymous audience. Here, the actors embrace this notion of creating a performative semaphore. Putting on their customers' clothing in an absurd, transformative way, Ching and Vera embody an array of attitudes. Each piece of clothing transforms the performer into a sculpture in motion.

stains. They'll put it in a bag and won't tell you. Maybe they think you won't take it?

   Ching puts a plaid skirt on her head.

VERA
The stains I think about the most are usually yellow. The shit you don't want to see, the shit you don't want to touch. You look for a plastic bag, you hold it like this, then you throw it in the hole, shut the door, and get out your quarters.

   Ching puts a small girl's pink dress over her face and looks through the tiny armhole.

VERA
See that guy, he's washing all these pairs of women's panties; black, red, pink, lots of lace, pretty sexy, and also kind of… big? I wonder who he's washing and folding them for, so carefully. I guess they're his wife's, or his girlfriend's, or his mom's. Or maybe they're just his.

   Ching wraps a green, slinky shirt over one arm, facing away.

VERA
Sometimes a customer, she'll come in and she'll say a certain thing is special and I wonder what special really means? They all say special. This blouse, or that skirt — it's really special, they'll say. For work or a date. It means be careful with it, or else.

   Drop-Off Customer returns, annoyed, and approaches Ching at the counter.

DROP-OFF CUSTOMER
Excuse me. It's still there.

CHING
Sorry, I tried —

DROP-OFF CUSTOMER
Look at that. Can you see it? Look, right there, right there.

CHING
I tried, but it's a tough one.

DROP-OFF CUSTOMER
Look at that... see that stain? Still there. You didn't try hard enough.

CHING
We tried our best.

DROP-OFF CUSTOMER
That's it. I'm not paying.

CHING
But, everything else... washed and folded. You have to pay.

DROP-OFF CUSTOMER
No! You didn't get it out. If it's not clean, I can't go to my job.

Vera turns on the TV, allowing us to see another documentary film segment with Jasmine, as herself, interviewing her grandmother Lula Holloway in her apartment.

We hear the filmmakers, Sachs and Olesker, off-screen.

Note: As part of her Wages for Housework movement in the mid-1970s, Silvia Federici developed a feminist theory of reproductive labor that recognized the economic value of domestic work, including laundry, as an indispensable component of a social economy. See Silvia Federici, "Wages against Housework (1975)," in *The Politics of Housework*, ed. Ellen Malo (London: Allison & Busby Limited, 1980), 253–61.

SACHS
I'm rolling.

OLESKER
And I'm recording. You can clap any time you're ready.

JASMINE
Okay, grandma. So, like I told you before, I'm working on this film project slash theater project, and it's centered around laundromat workers. Ok, so I came to you because I remember you telling me you worked in a laundromat before. Can you tell me about that?

A long awkward pause.

LULA
What? [laughter]

JASMINE
[laughter]

LULA
Yes, I worked in a laundromat from... I started in 1968.

JASMINE
Mm-hm.

LULA
Yes, I worked at the laundromat from... I started in 1968 and I was doing different types of work in the laundry. On the first floor, they washed the things and then they sent them up to the second floor and they would hang them. They would shake them and hang them, and put them on a hanger, and put them on the thing where they'd dry and they'd come out on the floor. And that's where different girls, you know, we had different people doing different things but, at the end, we were the last ones. Monday was light, Tuesday was heavy, Wednesday was light, Thursday was very heavy, and Friday was heavy. But it was very exciting, even though the pay wasn't too good.

JASMINE
Can I ask what the pay was?

LULA
I think I started off at $5-something an hour and, when I retired, it was $7.50 an hour, but I managed to survive. I learned how to live on my salary. I worked from 1968 to 1999 for the same company.

Note: The field recordings of laundromat interiors become music through the work of sound artist Stephen Vitiello. These aural elements include quarters being dropped into machines, water draining, the spin of a dryer, and people talking as they wait for their laundry.

Documentary film segment ends.

We hear the amplified sounds of rhythmic breathing.

Ching, Vera, and Jasmine repeat the T-shirt Dance, this time without actual clothing in their hands and using more compressed movement.

Jasmine moves away as Ching and Vera continue with these gestures, which become smaller and smaller. Ultimately, it transforms into a dance of only their fingers.

The Ghost Figure returns, a member of the Atlanta Washing Society of 1881.

GHOST FIGURE
We, the members of the Washing
Society, are determined to stand to
our pledge and make extra charges
for washing, and we have agreed,
and are willing to pay, $25 or $50
for licenses as a protection, so
we can control the washing for the
city. We can afford to pay these
licenses, and will do so before we
will be defeated. Then we will have
full control of the city's washing
at our own prices, just as the city
has control of our husbands' work
at their prices. Do not forget this.
We hope to hear from your council
Tuesday morning. We mean business
this week or no washing.

Yours respectfully,
The Washing Society, 486 Members

Shift to darkness.

*We hear an audio recording of two
women speaking in Chinese and
Spanish.*

Note: This collective letter was published in *The Atlanta Constitution* in July 1881. In her book *To 'Joy My Freedom*, Tera Hunter includes it as a primary document in her writing on the Washing Society, thus contextualizing the importance of this underrecognized yet extraordinary moment in American labor history: "In early July of 1881, twenty women and a few men met in a church in the Summerhill neighborhood [of Atlanta] to form a trade organization. After the meeting, the group instructed black ministers throughout the city to inform their congregations of a mass public meeting in another church. At the same time, they organized formally as the Washing Society, electing officers, appointing committees, designating subsidiary societies for each of the city's five wards and establishing a uniform rate at a dollar per dozen pounds of wash…. They established door-to-door canvassing as the mechanism to widen their ranks…. On July 19, the Washing Society members called a strike, in order to achieve higher fees at a uniform rate. The protest was the largest and most impressive among black Atlantans during the late 19th century." Tera Hunter, "'Washing Amazons' and Organized Protests," in *To 'Joy My Freedom: Southern Black Women's Lives and Labors after the Civil War* (Cambridge: Harvard University Press, 1997), 74–97.

Note: There is no English translation heard in this section of the performance. This is an attempt to replicate the experience that a non-English speaker might feel in the US. Here in this book, we do provide the English translation of the Chinese and Spanish text for you to read, but we encourage you initially to imagine just hearing the sound of the women's voices without translation.

VOICE/SPANISH:
No cámaras, por favor.
(No cameras, please.)

VOICE/CHINESE:
你永远不知道，坏主意。
(You never know, bad idea.)

No grabaciones.
(No recording.)

请让我一个人待着
(Leave me alone.)

Si te ven, te pueden atrapar... Si te ven...
(If they see you, they can catch you... If they see you...)

如果他们看到你，他们可能会抓到你。如果他们看到你...
(If they see you, they might catch you. If they see you...)

Dejé a mi familia allá, atrás.   我不得不去。
(I left my family behind.)   *(I had to go.)*

No tuve otra alternativa.
(I had no options.)

我来，是因为那儿没有工作了。
(I came because there was no work.)

La razón... el peligro. Porque era peligroso.
(The reason... it was so dangerous.)

Tenemos hambre.
那时我们饿了。
(We were hungry.)

A veces.
(Sometimes.)

一直很饿。
(All the time.)

Hubo una época en que teníamos de sobra, allá.
(It used to be that we had plenty, back home.)

很快，就吃不饱了。
(Soon there wasn't enough to eat.)

- 18 -

A very large film projection of brightly colored clothes spinning in a dryer appears on the wall of the performance space. Its presence is both abstract and specific.

我们很幸运现在有一份工作了。
(We're lucky to have a job now.)

La paga, no es muy buena – no es suficiente. ¿El salario mínimo? Es una broma. Usualmente, ni pienso en esto. Ya no.
(The pay, it's not very good – it's not enough. Minimum salary? It's a joke. I usually don't even think about it. Not anymore.)

No cámara, por favor. Ya no tengo nada más que decir.
(No camera, please. I have nothing more to say.)

请关闭相机吧。我无话可说。
(No camera, please. Nothing to say.)

Cuando llegué, tenía frío todo el tiempo. No importaba la temperatura, temblaba. Recuerdo que me regalaron un abrigo que alguien había dejado en un lugar en el que trabajaba. El jefe mismo me lo dio. Eso no es robar.
(When I got here, I was cold all the time. No matter the temperature, I was shivering. I remember being given a coat someone had left at a place where I worked. The boss gave it to me himself. That's not stealing.)

我有一张我家人的照片。
(I have one picture of my family.)

Usaba ese abrigo todo el tiempo. Incluso, cuando estaba adentro. Nunca sentí el calor suficiente como para quitármelo.
(I wore that coat all the time. Even when I was inside. I never felt warm enough to take it off.)

我把它别在这儿，我的夹克里，就在我的心旁边，你知道的。
(I kept it pinned here, inside my jacket, next to my heart, you know.)

Al principio venía a la lavandería. Olía bien. El "olor a limpio" me hacía sentir, usted sabe, mejor. ¿Pero, tú sabes cómo las cosas buenas no siempre lo son? Eran simplemente químicos..
(At first, I came to the laundry. It smelled good. The "clean smell" made me feel, you know, better. But, you know

how some good things are really not so good? They were really just chemicals.)

还有什么呢?一切我不记得。
(What else? I can't remember everything.)

No puedo olvidar nada.
(I can't forget anything.)

Vera and Ching enter, pushing laundry carts, fluid and dream-like. We watch them lit by the glow of the film projection as the voices in Chinese and Spanish continue.

We hear sparse, melancholy piano music against the rhythmic drop of coins in a laundry machine.

这儿现在是我的家,也不是我的家。我得小心一点儿。
(This is my home now, but it also isn't. I have to be careful.)

Uno no logra dejar de preocuparse pero, hay que hacerlo.
(You can't stop worrying, but you have to.)

Si dices demasiado, si se fijan en ti, si deciden buscarte, o averiguar tu estatus….
(If you say too much, if they notice you, if they decide to search or find out your status….)

如果你保持安静,去上班,回家,忙你自己的事,那就没问题。
(If you stay quiet, go to work, go back to your house, go about your business, then it's okay.)

Ella trabajaba todo el tiempo. Trabajaba para tanta gente. Distintos jefes. Lavando, cocinando, cuidando niños, cuidando ancianos. Así que… hay que tener cuidado.
(My friend had to leave, after she'd been here so long. And she worked all the time, for so many people. Different bosses. Washing, cooking, taking care of children, the elderly. So… you have to be careful.)

Presente… pero, ausente. ¿Tú sabes?
(Present… but also absent. You know?)

你微笑,说谢谢,我也说谢谢,你说再见,我也说再见。我一个人,但我并不孤单。我有你的衣服。它们是我在这里的原因,所以没有人会打扰我。
(You smile, you say thank you, I say thank you, you say goodbye, I say goodbye. I am alone but I am not alone. I

have your clothes. They are the reason I am here, so no one's going to bother me.)

   Jasmine enters, raises herself onto the folding table and lies down. Ching and Vera shake out a white sheet and gently place it over their sleeping co-worker, Jasmine.

El jefe no está aquí. Casi nunca está aquí y eso es bueno. Porque cuando estás aquí… vela todo lo que haces. Todo lo vela y todo le molesta. Se le nota en el rostro. En la forma en que te apunta con el dedo. Si eres lenta, o hablas demasiado….
(The boss is not here. He's hardly ever here, and that's a good thing. Because when he's here… he watches over everything you do. And everything annoys him. I see it in his face. The way he pokes his fingers at you. If you are slow, or if you talk too much….)

如果你忘记了什么….
(If you forget something….)

Si no puedes venir, o estás enferma.
(If you can't come, or you're sick.)

如果你洗的衣服不够多，如果你折叠得不够快。
(If you don't get enough loads done, if you don't fold fast enough.)

Efectivo. Me paga en efectivo, pero nunca suficiente. Es muy duro. Nunca es suficiente.
(Cash. He pays me in cash, but never enough. It's very hard. It's never enough.)

我不会说什么。我不能失去这份工作。如果我说什么，就是这样。
(I'm not going to say anything. I can't lose this job. If I said anything, that would be that.)

Una vez me dijo que me callara la boca. Puso la mano ahí y me moví deprisa. Él se rió.
(He once told me to shut up. He put his hand on me, and I moved away. He laughed.)

他有时会很好。他圣诞节时给了我额外的钱。每年都这样，总是这样。我想我很幸运。
(He can be nice sometimes. He gave me extra money at Christmas. He does every year, always. I guess I'm lucky.)

Él es dueño de varios lugares. Siempre viene a ver. Verifica el dinero. Tú sabes. A veces viene su esposa. Ella lo verifica todo también.
(The boss owns several places. He always comes to check. He checks the money. Sometimes his wife comes. She checks everything, too.)

Pero yo no digo nada. Me lo callo todo.
(But I try not to say anything. I keep everything inside.)

   Ching and Vera unfurl a string between them, revealing miniature shirts, dresses, and pants hanging on their tiny clothesline. The doll-sized clothes drift and sway in the air as the two women walk slowly towards the audience.

他们对我们很好。有时会请我们吃午饭。
(They're good to us. They buy us lunch sometimes.)

Nos dejan quietas, la mayoría del tiempo. Mientras hagamos nuestro trabajo, nos dejan quietas.
(They leave us alone, most of the time. As long as we do our job, they leave us alone.)

那么,你正在制作的这个东西是什么? Doc-u-mentary?
(So, what is this thing you are making? Doc-u-mentary?)

No cámara, no me graben, por favor.
(No camera, no recording, please.)

我为什么要让你?你的照片对我有什么帮助呢?
(Why should I let you? How will your pictures help me?)

Yo estoy AQUÍ, pero, esto AQUÍ no es mío.
(I am HERE, but this HERE is not mine.)

现在在拍吗?
(Is it running now?)

Tienes la cámara grabando.
(Is the camera running now?)

把它关掉。请关掉它吧。
(Turn it off. Turn it off, please.)

Quiero decirte que veas, pero, a la vez, no.
(I want you to see me, but, at the same time, no.)

   Projected film and audio recording ends.

Jasmine slowly gets up, holds the sheet in front of the table, and turns on a bright floor lamp, creating a shadow in silhouette of Ching and Vera who are now sitting at the table, hands folded. This feels like a formal interview, or an interrogation. The women now echo some of the same words that we heard in Chinese and Spanish in the last scene, translated and spoken in English, their gestures slightly exaggerated from behind the sheet.

VERA
No camera, please.

CHING
You never know — bad idea.

VERA
No recording.

CHING
Leave me alone.

VERA & CHING
No pictures. No record — please. If they see you, they might... you never know. Not safe, not sure. You never know.

VERA
I left my family back there.

CHING
I decided to leave.

VERA
I had no choice.

CHING
I came because there was no work.

VERA
And because it was too dangerous.

CHING
Not enough—

VERA	**CHING**
All the time.	Sometimes.

Jasmine suddenly drops the sheet and we see Ching and Vera pick up manila envelopes, remove the "documents inside," and begin reading.

VERA
It used to be that we had plenty —
tamarindo, guanabana, mamey, parcha, carambola… quenepa.
I don't even know how to say quenepa here. I can taste it, but I can't say it.

CHING
There was just not enough.

VERA
When I left, they were so young.
When they finally came, they were so much older.
When they came, I cried.

CHING
We're lucky to have jobs now.

VERA
But the pay? Minimum wage. Not even.

CHING
My kids have grown up here and now they're so different from me and how I grew up. They're mine, but they're different from me.

VERA / CHING
No camera.
Nothing more to say.

Pause.

VERA
When I first came, I was cold all the time. No matter what temperature, I was shaking. I remember they gave me a coat that someone had left in the place where I was working. The boss, he gave it to me.

CHING
I try not to forget anything.

VERA
I can still see my house.

CHING
It's so clear to me — and my street.

VERA
The tree that grew on the corner, the one with red flowers.
In English they call it Flamboyant tree, yes, Flam-boy-ant —
very flashy, right? Ha!

CHING
There was a bridge over the river.
Everyone walked over the bridge to get to work, school, to shop.
The river had so many fish but then it got very dirty.
The air has gotten so bad now.
I hear that most mornings you can hardly see at all.

VERA
Everything is different but also the same, only worse.

CHING
This is my home now, but it also isn't. I have to be careful.

VERA
You can't stop worrying, but you have to.

CHING
If you say too much —

VERA
If they notice you —

CHING
If they decide to look for you or into your status —

VERA
You pray everyone will be okay. I don't need anyone to help me with that. I can do it all on my own. Anywhere.

CHING
Sometimes I play a game with myself. These piles of clothes are a wall.

VERA
I pray when I'm working, lying in bed, riding the subway.
It's a way to pass the time.
My friend — she got sent back. She lived here for so many years.

CHING
I tell myself they're all here to protect me.

VERA
The boss isn't here right now. He's hardly ever here, which is good.
Cause when he is, he looks over you, watching everything and getting mad.
I can see it in his face.
The way he snaps his fingers,
if you're working too slow
or talking too much.

CHING
If you forget something –

VERA
If you're sick and have to go home –

CHING
If you don't get enough done.
If you don't go fast enough.
Cash.
He pays cash.
But not enough.

Ching and Vera leave.

On the TV, Ching appears on film. We see her face in close-up as she responds to an off-screen interviewer.

CHING
Chinese New Year and we were full of people washing their clothes, only not the kind of laundry we usually see, like big bags of sheets and family clothes... no, these were younger, maybe people in their twenties, and they're doing just a single pair of skinny pants or a shiny blouse to wear to a party, like they need to get just one or two things clean before going out to get drunk or something, you know? They just want to clean something quick to look good that night, you know?

The live performer Ching re-enters carrying a sheet. She observes herself on the TV. Her face on screen is as large as her whole body is in person.

One girl, a young woman, she is in a big hurry, like they all are. She throws her outfit into the machine, puts it on rapid and cold, then leaves to go to the store and get a cup of coffee or something. She comes back a little later, interrupts the cycle and...

Ching begins to twist the sheet, turning and stretching in relation to the material itself, both sensuous and emotionally wrought.

Bad for the machines, you know, breaks them down. And then, she comes over to me. I think maybe she knew I was watching her, and she asks me to watch her clothes for like a half hour or something, and says she will pay me five dollars for my attention. Then she just runs out the door, just like that. So, when I go to put her skinny pants and little blouse into the dryer, I see five wet one-hundred-dollar bills. Do you hear me? Five one-hundred-dollar bills! They must've fallen out of her pockets.

INTERVIEWER *(off camera)*
You're kidding!

CHING
And it was busy, like I said, with lots of customers, so no one noticed. Plus, when I saw that money, you know, I caught it real fast... like this.

Ching, on film, closes her fist.

INTERVIEWER
So what happened to it... the money?

CHING
What do you think?

Film segment ends.

Tony, a customer, enters and sits facing the audience.

TONY
They say you can tell a man by his clothes. I say you can tell a man by what's under his clothes.
The way he breathes, the beat of his heart, the thickness of his skin — you know what I'm saying?
But I used to have closets full. Oh yeah, very high-end stuff. Designer, top shelf, haute couture from Milan, London, you name it. Shanghai! Balinese shirts, Chinese silk, Indian linen, suits made to order. The finest cashmere. Paris cravats. Yeah!

Tony drifts away, listening to music on his headphones.

Jasmine holds up a few feet of clothesline between her hands. Vera moves several clothespins along the rope, as if calculating on an abacus. They are both in their own heads, doing the math yet somehow still working together.

Ching speaks to the audience.

CHING
I started working in a laundromat when I turned fifteen.
I'm sixty now.
So that's forty-five years.

And I work five or six days a week, six to seven hours a shift. And each day, I do about ten to fifteen loads of laundry so that's seventy loads a week, 280 a month, 3,360 a year. And then, over forty-five years, I have done 151,200 loads of laundry — or something like that — since I began. And then when I had babies, well, I was doing my own two times a week, that would be eight times a month, so that's seventy-eight loads, but wait a minute, each time I did it there would be two loads, wait, that's too much, so that's about seventy-two loads a week including the store loads, and my oldest child is forty-one now, so that would be 3,744 loads a year.

Is that possible? But wait...
Shouldn't I minus the loads that my son did himself when he turned fourteen or fifteen?
Yeah, I taught him something.

A shift.

JASMINE
What time is it?

CHING
Not time yet. Hours to go.

JASMINE
There are a few things you don't have to think about, like walking home at the end of the day.

CHING
It pulls you.

VERA
You just follow.

JASMINE
Right to your door.

VERA
Auto pilot.

JASMINE
Just wish it would end.

VERA
Close.

JASMINE
So we can go home.

CHING
What we call home here, anyway.

> The work day has come to an end. Each woman begins to sing her own song. We hear Ching singing in Tagalog, Vera in Spanish, and Jasmine in English. They all sing their separate songs at the same time, but each one can be distinctly heard.
>
> Tony returns.

TONY (*to the audience*)
I hate folding. I always have.
When I was married, my wife tried to show me. Drove her nuts.
What's wrong with you, she said.
Didn't anyone ever teach you anything?

> He opens a door to one of the machines.

Be careful of what's inside the machine, what's inside here. Don't you see it? The shadow. The shadow.

> Tony backs away, suddenly fearful.
>
> Film begins on the TV. We watch Jasmine, as herself, continue her interview with her grandmother Lula.

LULA
I think the union mostly worked with the bosses, because every time the representative would come there, you know, would come there to see about one problem, he'd always go away. He'd have a little meeting with us and say we're supposed to do this, we're supposed to do that — and a different one, every time. They switched up with the representative. They don't stay there long. They don't represent us too long. So, one day we went on strike because he owed us so much money. We went on strike one Friday until we got our back pay. And we had got bomb threats and things — you know, like that. Yeah, we had a picket line outside and I forgot who covered it, some news people who were there. And the second boss, he was peeping out the window to let the other boss know and he came in and they made the checks out. They gave everybody what they owed us because we had went before the union.

Film ends.

Music like the sound of water moving through pipes fades in.

Vera puts on red, latex-coated work gloves and goes to the folding table, making loud, rhythmic beats on its surface with her hands.

Tony puts on work gloves and holds his hands up in the air.

Ching puts on her gloves and raises her hands high above her head.

Together, they begin to do their own work-related gestures, building in speed and intensity, becoming more frenetic.

Jasmine holds up a pillowcase with the words "ATLANTA 1881" printed on it, and then wraps it around her body like an apron.

She addresses those gathered before her, delivering a public speech.

JASMINE
We come together now for higher pay, respect and autonomy, forming our own trade organization, which we call the Washing Society. There are just twenty of us, but we will

grow. We will establish a uniform rate of one dollar per dozen pounds of wash. Look around you now. This city has more home laundry workers than male common laborers, and that is a fact. We will hold a mass meeting and call a strike. We will go door-to-door, canvassing all over this city, and in just three weeks, our numbers will grow from 20 to 3,000 strikers.

We urge you to join or honor the strike: young and old, black and white. No matter if they arrest us, or fine us, let our proposed fees inspire you. We say to our City Council that we will pay those $25 licensing fees rather than be defeated.

We mean business this week, or no washing!

Ching goes to the table and Tony stands at the other side, a customer at her counter. He appears out of breath and very agitated.

TONY
I lost —

CHING
Hello. Can I help?

TONY
I lost a lot — Did you find — ? It was folded up in a rubber band.

CHING
Where was it?

TONY
In my pocket. A lot of money.

CHING
I didn't find it.

TONY
You must have. It was —

Note: Tera Hunter's writing provided essential historical material in the creation of Jasmine's role as the Washing Society member: "The effectiveness of the strikers, whatever their methods of convincing others to risk similar sacrifices, is borne out by the fact that their ranks swelled from 20 to 3,000 strikers and sympathizers within three weeks. The Washing Society maintained solidarity by meeting together almost nightly as one body or in decentralized ward divisions. Given the broad support and participation within the black community at large and the wide range of households outside that community that relied on manual laundry workers, the entire city was affected by this event. Communal laundry work, again, proved critical to facilitating this mobilization…. In the summer of 1881, their contestation took the form of a strike, not only because by then the prerequisite community institutions were in place, but also because of the broader political struggles and period of relative optimism that characterized the black community." See Hunter, *To 'Joy My Freedom*, 91.

CHING
Nothing there. Nothing at all. We give it back when we find it.

TONY
I don't believe you.

CHING
Did you look everywhere?

TONY
You took it. You took my money!

CHING
If I find any money, I return it, even if it's only one dollar.

TONY
I should call the police. Police! POLICE!

CHING
No, please, not here.

TONY
I will.

CHING
Don't call. Please, mister. No money here.

TONY
Are you calling me a liar?

CHING
Maybe someone else took it.

TONY
Who else could do that?

CHING
You left your things in the dryer a long time.

TONY
Are you saying it's my fault?

CHING
You go outside and did not come back... you fall asleep. Maybe someone else —

TONY
To hell with you. To hell with you people!

Tony leaves.

JASMINE *(to audience)*
It felt like I was underwater, in a machine turning around and around, and the water was rushing in, getting higher and higher, and I'm trying to find the window, like a ship's window, a portal. And the ocean is suddenly just swallowing me up and it's so cold, so salty, and I can't breathe. I'm wheezing and choking, but I reach for a piece of rope floating towards me. I'm trying to pull myself up, get my head above water. The white foam is everywhere, and big, ugly fish are swimming right up to me, staring into my eyes. And I'm thinking, how do they breathe, those fish? If only I had those things in my sides, those gills, instead of these lungs, so I wouldn't have this trouble. And one of those fish looks like it's about to take me in its mouth and swallow me up whole, but then I wake up and reach for the inhaler I keep right by my bed.

Ching and Vera move toward the audience.

CHING
See my wallet? There's nothing in it anybody would want.
Open it. Take a look.
I could leave it on the counter and I wouldn't care. I am who I am.
The last thing I need is worry. I worry all the time.
I come here, I try to keep busy.
I think about what I'm doing. I do a good job.
But most of the time, I still worry. I look at the clock at ten and I look again at noon.
I try not to look in between.

VERA
When I first came over the border, they took my fingerprints.

They said, "Press down here, on this document." I wasn't even sure what it was for, but I did it. I left a mark, forever.

Pause.

CHING
So what is this thing you say you are making?

VERA
A documentary? Of what?

VERA / CHING
No camera, no recording — please.

CHING
Why should I let you? What will it do — for us?

VERA
I'm here, but this *here*, this *place*, is not mine.
So I don't want you or anyone else in your group to take a picture of me here.

CHING
Is it running right now?

VERA
Do you have your camera going?

CHING
Turn it off. You can turn it off now, please.

VERA
They have a camera in here, too — for security. But is it safe?

CHING
We have to get back now — bye bye!

VERA
What is safe?

CHING
You want more?
Haven't we given you enough?

VERA
Turn it off now. What is that you say?

CHING
What is the word?

VERA
That's it. Over now!

CHING/VERA
Cut!!!

Ching and Vera turn away.

Jasmine offers a spoken word poem.

JASMINE
Before you, see
your mother,
wooden rack in the bathtub,
hung with stockings,
first washing machine and e-lec-tric dryer,
done almost every day,
a different pair of something clean, very clean.
And before her, your grandmother
with basin and wringer
boiling water in a tenement apartment, before that
there was me, post-civil war me, new dawn
taking in laundry for wages
for freedom of a kind
a long line hung
drying in the light
moving to before, but still
scrubbing on rock with sand, river flows
stick hits
back-breaking hot
for days on end
from the colonies and beyond
to whiten in sour milk rinse through fire ash before that
layers and layers of clothes
never washed
dried flowers and perfume cover
after the fullers of Ancient Rome, urine mixed with water
jump and stomp with bare feet
back to Egyptian
salt scrub
ancient sun-dried
keep going further and further
following that line of time
with only one fur scrap
on our back and to before that
when we first come into cold air
not yet wrapped but naked
so naked and clean

Film begins.

We see Brooklyn's Barclay Center Plaza. All four performers jump up together and exuberantly throw piles of laundry in the air then walk away, leaving the discarded clothing on the ground. Pedestrians pass by, seemingly oblivious to these cloth remnants.

Jasmine, the actor in her nineteenth-century costume, walks with determination across the frame, stepping over the pieces of clothing that have been left behind.

Film ends.

The performers break character and speak to the audience.

TONY
(As himself.)
So, I have a washer-drier now. I haven't been to the laundromat in years. But my washer broke, and the dirty underwear was piling up, so I had to go back. I hauled my bag of laundry down to the corner. I was even looking forward to seeing the lady there who always yelled at me for forgetting my ticket. It's one of those neighborhood places that you think will be here forever, something people will always need. It was one of the only places where you could still talk to strangers. But when I got to the corner, the laundromat was gone. In its place was an overpriced bakery with twelve-dollar slices of cake and seven-dollar pots of tea that you are not allowed to share.

CHING
(As herself.)
When I was growing up in a small town in the Philippines, we didn't use washers or dryers. Two women from the town would come once a week, very early in the morning, wrap the clothes in bed sheets in huge bundles, carry them on their heads, and walk to the river about two miles away, on the outskirts of town. As they washed, they would lay them on the rocks on the riverbank to dry. By the afternoon, they would return and the next day come back to do the ironing. Today, my family still doesn't use washers or dryers. The river has dried up, but we still have a washerwoman come once a week to hand wash, hang dry, and iron our laundry.

VERA
(As herself.)
I was hired to be a nanny but somehow ended up doing the laundry as well. One time, the mother left to do some grocery shopping and asked me to fold a pile of clothes "when I had a chance." The baby was crying, I was tired, and then I remembered the clothes! I hurry up the stairs with the baby and see three piles of clothes and I can't remember

which one I am supposed to fold so I grab whichever pile and fold them very neatly. A few days later, I return to work and she asks me to sit down. She seems very angry. She informs me that I folded all her dirty clothes and begins to question why I hadn't noticed what was dirty and what was clean. I remember just thinking that I honestly couldn't tell the difference.

JASMINE
(*As herself.*)
Who taught me how? My grandma did. She'd say to me, "Everything has to be done right. Everything has to be... to look... come out a certain way. You don't want those creases. You don't want not to have it right, you see?" She'd go on and on... it meant everything to her. She'd say, "you want it to look a certain way. And that's how you fold. You hold it like this, and then you pull it over like that. One-sies, Two-sies, Three-sies! Otherwise, it's not going to be right. It will come out all wrong. So pay attention to me now!"

Snaps her fingers.

"Listen! I am passing this down to you. Like my mother and her mother and... don't do it like that. Take your time. Make every fold matter. Put yourself into it. Like you mean it. Understand? Every fold counts. Do you understand? There. Like that."

We hear the sound of rhythmic breathing and music.

All performers move to the table. Their synchronous folding movements and ritual pounding on the surface of the table become an incantation. Together in a line, they raise their hands.

JASMINE
Hup!

VERA
Hup!

TONY
Hup!

CHING
Hup!

JASMINE
Hup!

Inhale.

End of play.

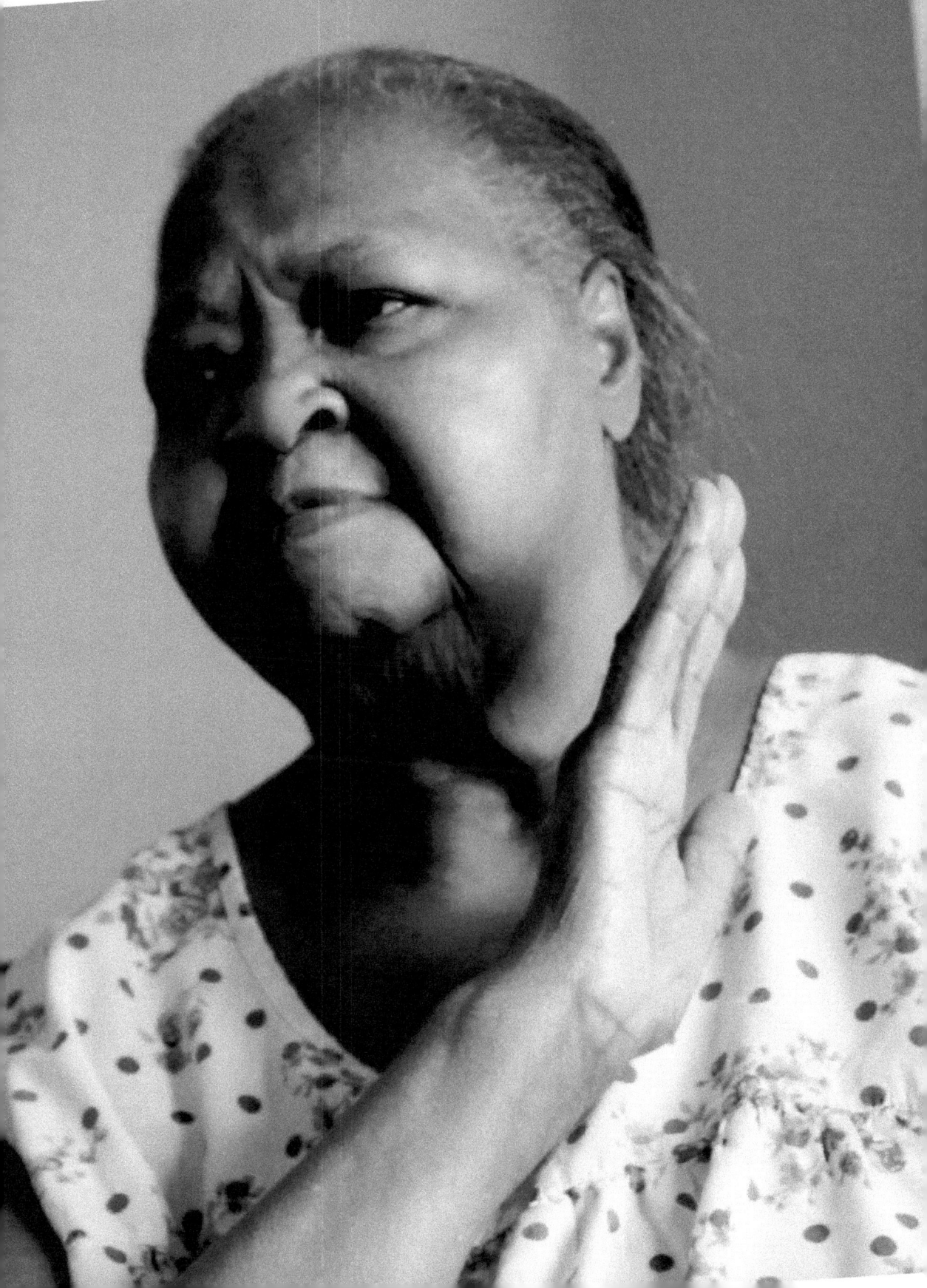

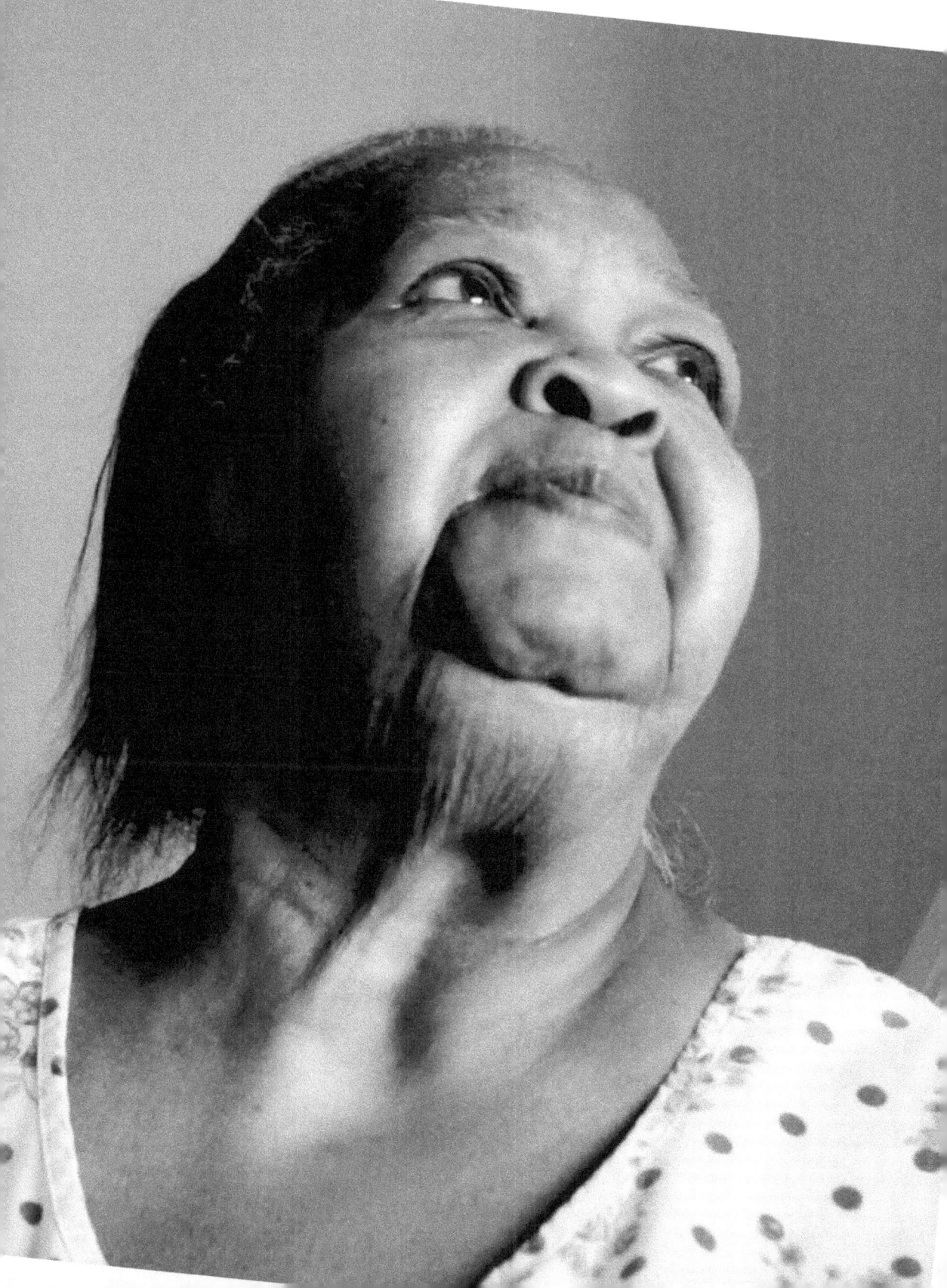

Taking on a Role

Jasmine Holloway

I remember being in my childhood apartment building, washing and folding clothes with my grandmother, Lula. She steadied my young, busy mind and hands by teaching me how to fold. I recall a time when Lula told me that she had worked in an actual laundry. My collaborators on the laundromat project were fascinated to hear this. They immediately encouraged me to interview my grandmother as part of our collective research. But when I asked her, she just said, "No."

I'm not sure how I wore her down, but she eventually answered my questions about her time working in the laundry. That being said, I should clarify something, or I'll let Lula do it: "I told you I didn't work in no laundromat!" I stood corrected and discovered that Lula worked at a commercial laundry center that helped supply and clean linens for different companies, restaurants, and such. She had worked in that laundry service, providing for her daughter (my mom), two grandchildren, and others for thirty years, from 1968 to 1999, making a little over $5 an hour.

My grandmother, Lulabelle Holloway, was more than the pieces of clothing she had to handle. Lula was a beautiful, creative, and compassionate woman, like many Black women before and after her. The safety, support, and love she deserved never should have been determined by her productivity. She was inherently worthy of a full and loving life just as she was. That's all that ever mattered. That interview helped me to start threading pieces of myself into this project.

***

As an actor, I was given the task of taking on the words of the Atlanta washerwomen of 1881. It wasn't until I was in the space performing in front of a live audience that I realized how the women must have felt back then—scared. Well, I know what that's like! To be afraid to do or say something, but frustrated enough to shout it out and get it done because there is no other way. Anyone from any marginalized group, especially a Black woman, knows what it feels like to demand respect—being angry and tired and scared all tumbled into… ENOUGH. We did many performances over the next several years. I finally got the words of the women of the Washing Society in my bones and in my spirit, and once I did, it felt really liberating.

* * *

I provided my own period costume for my role as a member of the Washing Society. I borrowed an old, long, grey skirt from a theater I worked in at the time. It was thick and brushed the ground as I walked. And for the top, a peasant cream blouse from Old Navy that I bought years ago. Wearing it was like layers on skin to me. Nothing more, nothing less. Even though the material of the skirt was hot and heavy against my body, I had a job to do. It was to embody the character of a Black washerwoman from the late 1800s. To me, that was all. As I walked to the set of the Brooklyn laundromat where we were filming that hot summer day, a man in a car suddenly sneered the words "Aunt Jemima" at me. I was quickly offended. I remember how that title was used to mock heavier black women such as myself: Aunt Jemima, the archetype of a Mammy, submissive and devoted. It's a caricature that's often haunted me but if I was paying closer attention that day, I would have realized that the woman that I was getting ready to portray—the very essence of her spirit which I was given the task to invoke—was anything but submissive.

May 14, 1881: "Arrest of a Washerwoman." Yesterday, Mrs. Osburn, who resides on Forsyth Street, caused the arrest of Anna Peters, colored. Anna had taken some clothes to wash for Mrs. Osburn, and failing to return them, was arrested. She was released on promising to appear to-day with either the clothes or the money to pay for them.

July 21, 1881: "The Washerwomen's Strike." The laundry ladies' efforts to control the prices for washing are still prevalent and no small amount of talk is occasioned thereby. The women have a thoroughly organized association and additions to the membership are being made each day. In the association there is a committee denominated the visiting committee, and the duties of this few is implied in the name. The visiting committee assemble at a designated place early in the morning, and after a consultation divide and spread themselves over the city. During the day the house of every colored woman who is not a member of the association is visited and a regular siege begun, and in nearly every instance an addition to the membership is the result. In this way the organization is continually growing, and the meetings, which are had every night, are largely attended and generally very demonstrative. The body has a regular corps of officers, and the conventions are up to style. Speeches advocating their rights and exhorting the members to remain firm are numerous and frequent. To several families whose washing left home Monday morning the clothing has been returned ringing wet, the women having become a member of the association after taking the washing away. It is rumored that house help is also on the eve of a strike.

July 26, 1881: "The Doughty Washwomen: Holding Out for an Advance in Wages." The washerwomen's strike is assuming vast proportions and despite the apparent independence of the white people, is causing quite an inconvenience among our citizens.

In one instance the demand for one dollar per dozen was acceded to. Those who decline to give this price are still wanting washers. Several families who decline to pay the price demanded, have determined to send their clothing to Marietta where they have secured laundry service. The strikers hold daily meetings and are exhorted by the leaders who are confident that the demands will be granted. The committees still visit the women and induce them to join the strike and when a refusal is met with threats of personal violence are freely indulged in to such an extent as to cause a compromise with their demands. There are some families in Atlanta who have been unable to have any washing done for more than two weeks.

Not only the washerwomen but the cooks, house servants, and nurses are asking an increase. The combinations are being managed by the laundry ladies.

FROM *THE ATLANTA CONSTITUTION*, 1881

July 29, 1881: "The Wet Clothes the Washerwomen Bring Home: The Story of the Organization Fully Told by Captain Starnes, Who Says a White Man and $300 Back the Strikers—The Way the Banks are Increased." Police court was well attended yesterday morning, and recorder Glenn added $186 to the city, treasury by fines imposed.

Among other cases, the disposed of were those against Matilda Crawford, Sally Bell, Carrie Jones, Dora Jones, Ophelia Turner, and Sarah A. Collier. This sextette of ebony hued damsels was charged with disorderly conduct and quarreling, and in each case, except the last, a fine of five dollars was imposed and subsequently paid. In the case of Sarah A. Collier, twenty dollars was assessed and the money not being paid, the defendant's name was transcribed to the chain gang book, where it will remain for forty days.

Each of these cases resulted from the washer women's strike. As members of that organization, they have visited women who are taking no part in the strike and have threatened personal violence unless their demands were acceded to, and their example followed. During their rounds they met with persons who opposed the strike and who declined to submit their proposition to become members. This opposition caused an excessive use of abusive and threatening language and the charge of disorderly conduct and quarrelling was the result.

Soon after court a Constitution representative heard Captain Starnes remark, "Well, Glenn's a good one; he put the fine on the strikers, and tomorrow we will have additional subjects for his consideration." This remark caused the reporter to ask Starnes if he knew what he was talking about.

"Of course I do," was the reply. "Bagby and I have been working on this matter ever since the strike began, and if anybody in town knows anything about, I guess we do."

"Well, tell us what you know."

"Well, you see this society was first organized about one year ago. The first meeting was held in the church on Summer Hill, but only a few women attended. They tried hard to get up a strike, but could not succeed and the thing soon broke because nobody would join. This year however, they have been successful and today nearly 3000 negro women are asking their white friends who supported them during the cold, hard winter to pay them a dollar a dozen for washing."

"You say they organized a year ago?"

"Yes, but that organization went to pieces. The society that now exists is about two weeks old. Next Saturday night three weeks ago, twenty negro women and a few negro men met in Summer Hill church and discussed the matter. The next night the negro preachers in all the churches announced a mass meeting of the washerwomen for the following night at Summer Hill church. The meeting was a big one and the result was an organization. Officers were elected, committees appointed and time and places for meeting read out. Since then, there has been meetings every night or two, and now there is a club or society in every ward in the city and the strikers have increased from twenty to about 3000 in less than three weeks."

"What do they want at these meetings?"

"Make speeches and pray. They swear they never will wash another piece for less than one dollar a dozen, but they will never get it, and will soon give in. In fact, they would have caved before this, but for the white man who is backing the strike."

"Do you know that there is a white man behind these strikes, or is it a rumor?"

"I know it, and I'll tell you who it is if you want to know."

"No, never mind his name. Tell me how you know."

"I have heard it from several responsible parties. There is Dora Watts, who lives at Mr. Wolfe's, 144 Jones Street, who swears that a white man addressed a meeting last week. She also says that he will speak to them next Monday night. This man tells them that he will see them through all right. They have a fund of $300 and feel confident of getting what they ask."

"They are trying to prevent those who are not members from washing, are they not?"

"Yes. The committee first goes to those who have no connection with the organization and try to persuade them to join. Failing in this, they notify them that they must not take any more washing at less than one dollar a dozen, and then threaten them with cowhides, fire and death if they disobey. Out on Walker Street, there lives a white lady, a Mrs. Richardson, who has had but one washer woman for eight years. Her name is Sarah Gardner. Her husband joined the strikers, and would not let his wife take the washing. Mrs. Richardson hired another woman who took her clothes away Monday, but brought them back in the afternoon, saying that the 'committee wouldn't let her wash for less than a dollar a dozen.' Mrs. Richardson, then induced a girl she had in the house to undertake the washing, but yesterday evening, while she was at work on Mrs. Richardson's place, a committee composed of Dora Shorter, Annie King, and Sam Gardner came up and threatened to kill her if she didn't stop, and when the lady, Mrs. Richardson, came out and ordered them away, they refused to go, and began to abuse her. I heard of it and now all three are in there, and Spyres has the key. He is fond of locking, but hates to unlock a door. I guess Recorder Glenn will catch 'em for $20 each."

"So they are on their muscle?"

"Well, I should say so. The men are as bad as the women. When a woman refuses to join the society, their men threaten to 'whip 'em,' and the result is that the ranks are daily swelling. Why, last night there was a big meeting at New Hope Church, on Green's Ferry Street, and fifty additions were made to the list. They passed resolutions, informing all women not members of the society to quit work, or stand the consequences. I tell you, this strike is a big thing, but if Glenn will only stand up to Bagby and myself, we will break it up. I am going to arrest everyone who threatens any woman, and I am going to try to get the chain gang full. Then they will stop. Why, let me tell you, out here on Spring Street is an old white woman who lives over her washtub. The infernal scoundrels went to her house yesterday, and threatened to burn the place down and to kill her if she took another rag. Emma Palmer, Jane Webb and Sarah Collier, with two white women, are doing the work, but I think Spyers will get a chance to lock 'em up before dark."

July 30, 1881: "The Washerwomen." Dora Shorter and Annie King, two more of the belligerent washerwomen, were yesterday before Recorder Glenn for trial. The charge against the duet was disorderly conduct and quarreling and the evidence sustained the charge. Recorder Glenn imposed a fine of twenty dollars against each, and in disposing of the cases said: "In these cases, I will impose a fine of twenty dollars upon each of the defendants, but hereafter, when the evidence is as conclusive as it is here, I will punish the offenders by sending them to the city chain gang."

August 3, 1881: "The Washing Amazons: They Grow Firm and Promise to 'Stick'." Among other resolutions passed by the City Council Monday night was one imposing a license of $5 per annum upon all washerwomen who belong to any organization having for its object an excessive pay for work.

This action of the council has fallen like a bombshell in the camps of the strikers and has induced quite a number to withdraw from the organization. There are many, however, who laugh at the resolution, and say emphatically that they will neither give in nor pay license. Of this latter class there is a majority, and that they are willing for the world to know just how their stand is evidenced by the following letter received by Mayor English yesterday:

WASHING SOCIETY, Atlanta, Ga., August 1—

Mr. Jim English, Mayor of Atlanta—Dear Sir:

We, the members of our society, are determined to stand to our pledge and make extra charges for washing, and we have agreed, and are willing to pay $25 or $50 for license as a protection, so we can control the washing for the city. We can afford to pay these licenses and will do it before we will be defeated, and then we will have full control of the city's washing at our own prices, as the city has control of our husband's work at their prices. Don't forget this. We hope to hear from your council Tuesday morning. We mean business this week or no washing.

Yours respectfully,

From 5 Societies, 486 Members.

Last evening there was a big meeting of the organization on Wheat St. It is estimated that fully 500 women and men were present, and the action of the council was made the feature of the evening. It was discussed by the men and women, and many of the speeches were of the most "expressive" character. They openly denounced the council for imposing the tax and defied an attempt to collect the same. But this spirit of bravado was not entertained or manifested by all. Quite a number advocated a compromised measure and intimated an intention to seek work at any price.

The strike, thanks to Recorder Glen, Bill Starnes and Connolly, has about reached its finale, and in a week at the furthest the washerwomen will be bending over their tubs singing songs as loudly as if they had succeeded.

With Atlanta's people the question is a leading one as a topic of discussion. Our businessmen are astonished at the colored people's stupidity in not seeing that they are working their own ruin. In a short time, winter will be again upon them, and they will once again be calling for aid. Many gentlemen say that when this time comes, and it will surely come, they will refuse to give anything towards sustaining those who now decline to work for fair remuneration.

One gentleman, whose washerwoman is his tenant, was told by her that she could not wash any more for less than a dollar a dozen. "All right," said the gentleman, and the woman started off, happy in the thought that she had succeeded, but just as she reached the door with the clothing the gentleman said: "Mary, I have decided to raise my rent. Hereafter you must pay me $25 per month rent." "Why?" asked the woman. "Because," said the merchant, "you have gone up on washing. I will go up on house rent." The woman agreed to take the washing at the usual price.

And here is another feature for the strikers. If they persist in their exorbitant demands, they will find house rent going up so rapidly that they will have to vacate.

A HOLE IN HISTORY: IN CONVERSATION WITH TERA W. HUNTER

Tera Hunter's book *To 'Joy My Freedom: Southern Black Women's Lives and Labors after the Civil War* (Harvard University Press, 1997) gives a rare glimpse into a brief period in American history when a group of Black women who called themselves the Washing Society became empowered through their collective actions. The book uncovers a story of working class women that is rarely told. It would have been impossible for us to build a connection between New York City's laundromat workers of today and laundry workers of the past without Hunter's book on the Atlanta washerwomen from 1881. She captures this moment in labor history through a vivid portrayal supported by crucial primary source material. Her dramatic retelling of meetings in churches, door-to-door organizing, and the eventual call for a city-wide strike provided a jumping off point for us.

Hunter's influence on our work became even more evident at a very specific moment: when we were making the final decision for the title of our film. We knew that we would only call it *The Washing Society* if we contacted her directly, shared our work-in-progress, and heard her thoughts. Not only did Hunter give us her support, but she also invited us to premiere our film at "To 'Joy: A Symposium on Black Feminist Histories," a celebration of the 20th anniversary of the publication of her book at the Carter G. Woodson Institute at the University of Virginia.

We interviewed Tera Hunter in 2022.

Lizzie: *Now, years later, thinking about your book and the story of the Washing Society, we were wondering if the historical research you're doing is shaped by the time you're in? I know it was a while back for you, over twenty years ago. How was your writing and research shaped by what was going on in the world at that time?*

Tera: At the time, I was really interested in figuring out a way to do the history of working-class women, because very little had been written about black working-class women in particular, and even not much more had been written about white working-class women. So the washerwomen's strike became an entry into figuring that out. I was very much influenced in terms of where women's history and working-class history were at the time. I was doing my research into the silences and absences. I wanted to know more about the lives of ordinary people.

I was going through my files and I realized that I had written an epilogue to the book that I did not use. It was the story of Dorothy Bolden, who became one of the leading activists for domestic workers in the 1970s in Atlanta, Georgia. Actually, I did a piece for *The New York Times* a few years ago when Stacey Abrams first ran for governor, and domestic workers were a part of her support group. They were out in the streets of Atlanta and in the suburbs, organizing door-to-door on her behalf. So I wrote a piece putting those histories together.

Lynne: *Could you talk about the finding of the original articles on the Washing Society of 1881 in* The Atlanta Constitution, *that moment when you first discovered the material?*

Tera: Well, I actually came across it because two other historians had written about it. So I didn't discover it from scratch. Neither one of them had written about it fully. Howard Rabinowitz, a historian of the urban South, wrote about it in a very dismissive way, I would say, in his book *Race Relations in the Urban South.* Jacqueline Jones wrote about it in her *Labor of Love, Labor of Sorrow: Black Women, Work, and the Family from Slavery to the Present.* She created a more positive portrayal, but still didn't fully write about it. Those books were my starting points, but then I realized there was a lot more there than either of them had paid attention to. So that's how I got to *The Atlanta Constitution,* and what I discovered supported a much wider view of these women and how effective they were even though, in the long run, they still remained poorly paid workers.

Lynne: *And that's where you found the women's speeches and their letters.*

Tera: Yes.

Lynne: *Your work as a historian has inspired many cultural responses in many forms. What resonances do you see in the dialogue between history and art?*

Tera: Well, I think there are so many possibilities. Is there ever a point at which art isn't in dialogue with history in some way or another? Even when it's not explicitly so, it's still calling attention, perhaps, to an absence there. I think about poetry, music, film, theater, and visual art. Artists like author Thulani Davis, composer Nnenna Freelon, visual artist Maya Freelon, and playwright a.k. payne have all been engaged with the broader issues my work addresses. Also, more specifically, they have explored my work on the washerwomen in Atlanta and working class women in general.

Each of these artists also helped me to see my work in a different way.

Lynne: *The breadth of your influence became even clearer during the Woodson symposium when we heard scholars such as Crystal Feimster and Robin D.G. Kelley speak on your work. Your research and writing on the Washing Society has also been a muse for politicians like Elizabeth Warren and labor groups like the AFL–CIO. This is especially true in terms of your focus on collective actions, particularly women's. It took the world many years since the publication of your book in 1997 to finally recognize this moment in history.*

Tera: That's a good point. It is interesting how, in recent years, people have found this story and how it is such an inspiration, because people assume that way back then, these women would not have been able to organize the way that they did, on their own behalf. So, they provide a really good example for thinking about our own times. If they could have done what they did in 1881, then why can't people in the twenty-first century do something similar?

Back when I was trying to publish the book, my editor was very supportive, but the press was very skeptical. They didn't think it was going to sell. They thought it was too academic and didn't have the potential to reach a broader audience. And yet, it really found all kinds of readers. I've had some of my most interesting conversations with people who just found my book outside of the academy.

A group of women in Columbia, South Carolina, for example, created this whole event around the book and invited me to come and talk about it. They had never done anything like that before. Or, there were the fourth graders that I spoke to in a private girls' school in Maryland, where their teacher introduced them to the Atlanta washerwomen's strike. I had the chance to listen to their reactions and their own stories that they told me.

Lynne: *That's fantastic. Teaching fourth-grade girls to collectivize and organize.*

Tera: Exactly. They were all for the washerwomen. They were definitely on their side.

Lizzie: *This group of women, who were not seen historically, had agency. They acted collectively in their own interest, which is so powerful. Part of what I think makes your book extraordinary is how you're both this historian bringing out all this information, but also you tell a compelling story. It reads as this very engaging, almost dramatic narrative, while still having this truth and fact-based research. When we read about the Washing Society and the strike, we see the world* *and ourselves differently. The absence or silence that you talk about addressing is suddenly given voice and presence. It's the truth that's been hidden.*

Lynne: *Do you think that scholars and artists can, or should, approach historical truths differently?*

Tera: How do we get to what we each understand as truth, as historical truth? Our forms influence the method and the sources that we use, how we tell the stories. Of course, artists are much freer in terms of how they can express and articulate what historical truth means, what your understanding of it is. But I think artists are still accountable. What is or is not in the piece? What's the angle? What's the perspective? Whose perspective are you telling and what are you highlighting? I think we come at it differently, but ultimately, I think integrity behind the work is what I see as critical.

Because it was too dangerous.

I left my family behind.

I came because there was no work.

In Praxis: A Bridge Between Art and Activism

with Rosanna Rodríguez and Mahoma López

How did our project connect with the actual organizing efforts of laundromat workers?

Mahoma López and Rosanna Rodríguez, co-directors of the Laundry Workers Center, contributed to our process from the beginning. We initially connected with them while conducting our research and this developed into an ongoing exchange of ideas. Over the years, we took part in their workplace protests, which we documented in the videos *Despertar* and *Sunshine Laundry Action*, both of which have since been used in the Laundry Workers Center's outreach.

López and Rodríguez have also talked about their crucial organizing efforts after screenings of our film in New York City at Anthology Film Archives, DCTV (Downtown Community Television), and Metrograph Cinema. Here we share the Laundry Workers Center mission statement, followed by the personal narratives of López and Rodríguez:

> *The Laundry Workers Center addresses the need for community-based leadership development geared toward improving the working and living conditions of workers in the laundry, warehouse, and food service industries, as well as their families. We aim to combat abuses such as landlord negligence, wage theft, and hazardous and exploitative working conditions, all of which are endemic in low-income communities in New York City and New Jersey.*
>
> *Laundry Workers Center's political philosophy is rooted in organizing workers and building their leadership skills and political power through a variety of worker-led tools and tactics, including taking direct action at the workplace, serving as their own voice to media outlets, speaking out as members of the community, and acting as their own advocates at the negotiation table.*
>
> *In 2011, we decided to organize the retail and coin-operated laundromat industry because we observed the precarious working conditions and the fact that there wasn't any organizing happening. While laundromats are public spaces, the workers suffer from isolation.*

We often work with female laundromat employees to help them recognize their rights as workers and as women. The workforce in NYC and NJ are immigrant women of color, and the working conditions are deplorable. Many are victims of wage theft, discrimination, safety hazards, sexual harassment, and physical abuse.

In 2018, we launched our first organizing campaign in East Harlem where we fought against TYS Laundromat. After a year in the struggle, we won this campaign by guaranteeing a 40-hour week, overtime pay, a punch clock system, and back wage settlement for the workers. Our second labor campaign was in Brooklyn against the Sunshine Shirt Laundry Center which had committed wage theft, health and safety violations, and physically abused workers. We won that campaign in 2020.

We also developed the leadership of six Hispanic women who participated in our program. They have now formed an independent union certified by the National Labor Relations Board. We also worked with members of the Liox Wash Supply Campaign who then achieved a vital step: the Department of Labor certified their U-Visas because of the labor abuses these women suffered in their workplace.

We saw many laundromat workers get sick during the Covid-19 pandemic. After struggling to work without proper PPE and using paper towels as a mask, our member Beatriz contracted COVID and was unjustly fired. She led her campaign and got her job back as well as her lost wages. Many workers have a similar story.

We need to bring to light all of these issues to combat inequality.

Mahoma López

Soy de México, del Distrito Federal, y llevo 23 años en este país. Rememorando mis épocas de bachillerato, recuerdo que una maestra nos ofreció darnos puntos para la clase si entrevistábamos a los Zapatistas (EZLN), que para esa época habían ocupado el Zócalo en la ciudad de México.

En ese entonces era muy joven y de ciudad y, en parte por ignorancia, me preguntaba para qué me serviría hacer esto. Pero lo hice y tuve la oportunidad de ir varias veces y hablar con ellos. A raíz de esos intercambios comencé a entender la desigualdad que hay en nuestras propias comunidades indígenas. Es una lástima porque el sistema nos enseña a olvidarnos de nuestros orígenes, y muchas veces no nos damos cuenta.

Por razones del destino tuve que emigrar a este país. Yo pensaba que al ser un país del primer mundo no existirían esas desigualdades, pero me sorprendió sobremanera darme cuenta de cómo se trata a las personas aquí, especialmente a los inmigrantes. Al llegar a este país sin saber hablar inglés el primer trabajo que pude conseguir fue de lavaplatos en un restaurante. Ser lavaplatos es uno de los trabajos más difíciles que hay. Trabajé en esta industria por muchos años y mi experiencia fue una de mucha explotación, discrimen y constante abuso verbal.

En el 2011, cansado de tanto abuso, comencé a explorar otras alternativas y fue cuando me di a la tarea de buscar organizaciones que pudieran ayudarme. La experiencia fue tan buena que decidí convertirme en organi-

zador laboral. Al ser parte de Laundry Workers Center, he conocido muchas groupos y gente increíble de todas partes. Nosotros contribuimos a organizar un sector olvidado. Recordemos que la lucha de las trabajadoras de lavandería en este país data desde 1800, y hasta el sol de hoy siguen siendo abusadas. La verdad es que no hay mucho material o historia sobre estas trabajadoras.

Un día nos invitaron a ver la película The Washing Society sobre los trabajadores de lavandería. Nos pareció interesante así que decidimos ir. Cuán grande fue mi sorpresa al escuchar del increíble trabajo que estas compañeras trabajadoras habían hecho y sus relatos. Además, la forma artística como lo presentaron me hizo comprender que para organizar también se usa el arte.

Este documental sin duda fue una herramienta de aprendizaje y de inspiración y damos gracias a las compañeras por apoyar el trabajo de Laundry Workers Center y las trabajadoras de lavandería y dejar plasmado en video estas hermosas luchas de la clase trabajadora.

I am from Mexico, Federal District, and I have been living in this country for 23 years. Thinking back on my high school years, I remember a teacher who offered to give us extra points in her class if we interviewed the Zapatistas (EZLN), who at that time had occupied the Zócalo square in Mexico City.

I was very young and from the city, so at that time I remember asking myself, in part from ignorance, what would be the purpose of doing that? But I went and had the opportunity to go several times to talk with them. Because of those exchanges, I started to understand the inequality that exists in our own indigenous communities. It's a shame because the system teaches us to forget about our origins, and we are often not conscious of this.

As fate would have it, I had to emigrate to this country. I thought that, being a first world country, these inequalities would not exist here. But I was very surprised to watch how people are treated here, especially immigrants. When I arrived in this country, without any knowledge of English, the first job I could find was as a dishwasher. Being a dishwasher is one of the most difficult jobs. I worked in this industry for a long time. My experience was one of exploitation, discrimination and constant verbal assault.

In 2011, tired of so much abuse, I began exploring other options and I started to look for organizations that could help me. The experience was so good that I decided to become a labor organizer. By being part of the Laundry Workers Center, I've come into contact with so many groups and incredible people from all around the world. We contribute to the organization of a forgotten sector. Let's remember that the struggle of laundry workers in this country dates from 1800, and they still continue to be abused. The truth is that there is not much material or history about these workers.

One day, we were invited to watch the film "The Washing Society" about laundry workers. We thought it was interesting so we decided to go. It was a great surprise to listen to the incredible work that these comrade workers had done and their stories. Plus, the artistic way in which it was presented led me to understand that to organize, you can also use art.

HAND BOOK

> *This documentary was, without a doubt, a learning and inspirational tool and we thank you for supporting the work of the Laundry Workers Center and the laundry workers, and for being able to portray in video the wonderful struggles of the working class.*

Rosanna Rodríguez

I am an immigrant, Latinx woman, and a mother of two from the Dominican Republic. I was born in a Catholic family, and when I was 12 years old, I became involved with a group from my church, La Pastoral Juvenil. The group was not about religion. It was more about bringing youth together in a very dynamic way to discuss many topics, meeting once a week. I started as a participant, then became the group leader, and eventually I was part of the steering committee. I believe this experience planted a seed that grew over time and helped me raise my voice in the face of injustice.

I migrated here to the United States in 2010 and in my first job I got paid by the day, not per hour. I was not verbally abused or mistreated, but I suffered wage theft and discrimination because I was pregnant. My boss told me, "You have to think about what you are going to do because you don't know if your child will be healthy." All of this made me think about workers' rights and organizing. My husband Virgilio and I started thinking about the foundation of an organization where we would centralize workers. The idea was born to create the Laundry Workers Center. We invited some friends and we started our journey.

It was hard! We worked day and night. We knocked on many doors because nobody knew the organization. We went to many events and meetings so that people knew about the organization's existence, and my husband and I spent all our savings. I have to confess that at the beginning I was afraid. I didn't feel sure about what we wanted to do. We didn't have any space for our meetings, and we didn't have resources. In 2012, during the Hot & Crusty food service organizing campaign, we had to meet in a McDonald's and in other cafes. We sacrificed a lot, but it was worth it because we did it with our hearts and committed ourselves to our principles and mission.

As a woman, this process was a big challenge. I had only been living in this country for two years. My first son was two months old, and I was learning to be a mom with my immediate family far away from me.

Being part of the Laundry Workers Center has changed me. I see the world through the stories of members, workers, and leaders. On many occasions, I have witnessed how our philosophy, strategies, and tactics are effective. Organizing requires much effort, but it is rewarding and fills me with great joy. Many members have gone through our leadership institute, and their transformation is 360 degrees. Like other colleagues, I was a volunteer for a long time, helping to organize, and when the opportunity arose, I became co-director. At some point, another member will take my position.

On some occasions my life, as well as my family's, has been threatened. Unscrupulous employers have sued us, but still we continue to fight for justice and for a better future for our children. I am proud to work with a team that fights for respect and equality for all, and change within the labor movement. Often, we don't realize that we have been educated in this system of vertical hierarchies. We have to be self-critical. If we are not, then we will be part of the bureaucracy. If we want to achieve something, we must do it as a collective. Real solidarity is required to build a strong movement. It's what we need to give power to the workers.

Scan here to see the video "¡Despertar!: New York City Laundry Workers Rise Up":

shake, rattle, and...

Stephen Vitiello

I do love the sound of a good washing machine, particularly with the build-up to the rattle and shake of the wash cycle. Our home washing machine sits on an imbalanced floor. Recently, the bounce became strong enough that the whole thing shifted. We can feel the vibration throughout the house. On a good day, I notice that certain percussive details come through. The pulse of the wash cycle also echoes a bit more as it hits the resonance of some metal in our pipes and maybe the glasses sitting on top of the refrigerator. When the vibration is strongest, they all ring out like they're singing.

While I was working on the soundscape for the performance *Every Fold Matters* and later, the film *The Washing Society*, I asked a friend and sound recordist to capture field recordings for me in a Brooklyn laundromat. I worried things might not be quite the same in Richmond, Virginia, where I live, and that it would be better to have New York City authentically represented. Those recordings became the foundation for my sampling, looping, and layering. I was thinking about a scene in a film I had seen where the background sounds of machines become foregrounded and blend into the rhythms of songs and then take center stage.

One could call a laundromat a small cathedral. There is a sound to a space created by the people who fill it: the acoustics—dampened by all the fabric—speaking or not speaking, whispering, paperback pages being turned, or just hands clicking keys on cell phones. I imagine that most people working in laundromats tune it all out, but there is an ensemble feel as one machine churns and another swirls. The chugging rhythm plays against the wash of other machines. Then there's the sound of all the coins collected and put into slots, the soft sounds of folding, and the murmur of voices.

SOUND OF A MACHINE DOOR CLOSING

Amanda Katz

Editing is about finding rhythms between shots, motion, sound, and language. There is no shortage of these elements in a laundromat. I try to draw this out through both the performative and verité material in a film. Attention is given to the specificity of the actions that go into the process. Inside a laundromat, where machines are always turning on and off and customers are entering and exiting, our baseline "room tone" is constantly shifting. When an actor, worker, customer, or owner pauses while folding or stops speaking, I punctuate their action with the sound of a machine door closing or a spin cycle stopping or starting.

My experience editing *The Washing Society* made me notice who's working at the laundromat, who does their own laundry, and who drops it off. These questions revealed the subtleties in how COVID-19 in particular impacted the city.

In the apartment where I lived during the pandemic, I could see the local laundromat directly across the street from my window. It remained open for the first few weeks, then closed for six months. I stopped going there early on for fear of the virus and chose to start doing my laundry by hand. I was out of work and unable to do anything but consume the news. I washed a few things almost daily in the tub, but I never felt like I could get all of the detergent out.

I'm back to using the laundromat again and for a few weeks I watched the Euro Cup with my Polish neighbors on a very small TV while all of our clothing was turning, spinning, and drying together.

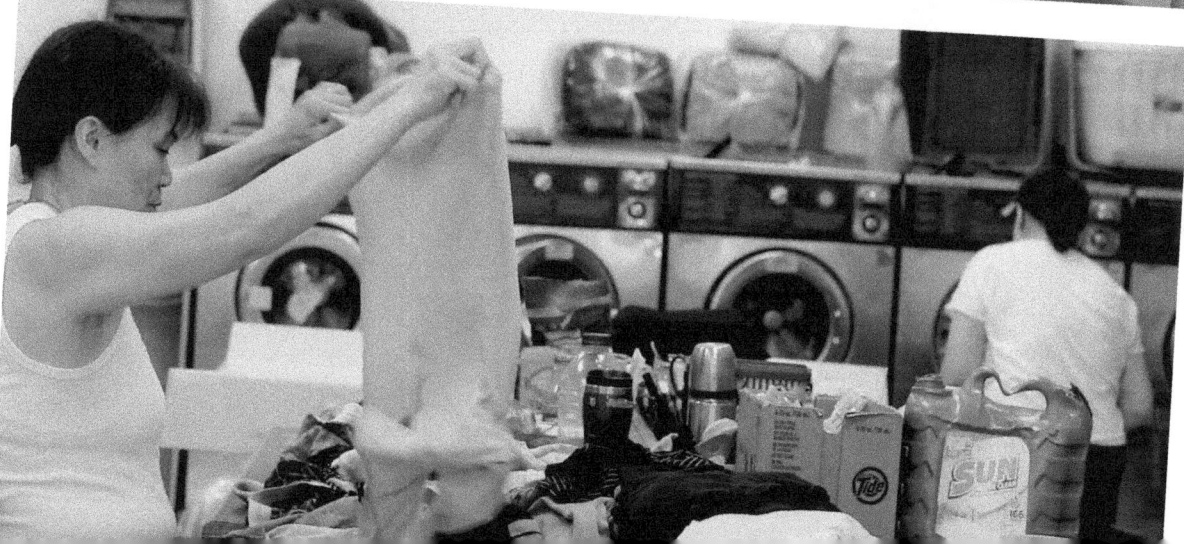

service, not servitude

Andrea Estepa

The essential labor of cleaning and cooking and caretaking, when done for money rather than out of love or personal obligation, is underpaid, often disdained, and left to those at the bottom of our social and economic hierarchies: women (particularly women of color) and recent immigrants. As a historian, I think about the ways that "service work" serves as a gloss for "servitude." To not have to do your own laundry is a privilege. Is that why the people who do it are so often seen as "less than"? Is the person who cleans up the mess by definition inferior to the person who makes it?

Lynne Sachs and Lizzie Olesker's film *The Washing Society* rejects the linear approach of traditional documentary as it captures an element of laundry work that echoes from the nineteenth century to the twenty-first. The statements of contemporary laundry workers that are woven through the film emphasize the routinized nature of the labor—tasks are repetitive, and every day is like any other. They make the work sound mechanical. An image of a hand putting quarter after quarter into a slot captures the connection of body to machine. Some customers treat the workers more like machines than people: Margarita Lopez, a worker interviewed in the film, describes how they drop off their clothes with "not even a hello, not even a good morning." The customers' sense of entitlement in contemporary New York City is not unlike that of nineteenth-century Atlantans. Continued discrimination in education and employment based on race, gender, and citizenship means that we find women of color doing domestic labor—whether in private homes or industrialized settings—140 years after the Atlanta washerwomen's strike. By connecting the experiences of today's laundry workers in New York City to those in Atlanta in the 1880s, *The Washing Society* creates a space where we can ponder what has changed and what hasn't about this work through the people who do it. In the opening scene, actress Jasmine Holloway portrays an 1880s laundress describing her labors, and in the next she is seated in a contemporary laundromat as two women—her professional descendants—arrive to start their workday. What does she observe? Today's laundry workers—most of the ones we see are Asian and Latina, not African American—have access to modern technologies the original Washing Society could not have imagined. The washing is done by machine, not by hand, and they don't have to carry water or make their own cleaning supplies from scratch. But the work is still physically demanding. The members of today's "washing society" are always on their feet, bending and lifting, heaving laundry bags that can weigh anywhere from one pound to one hundred pounds, and forever folding, folding, folding. It can be backbreaking: Lopez tells us she developed a herniated disc since starting her job at the laundromat. We think of "women's work" as not requiring as much strength as "men's work." Whether in the nineteenth or the twenty-first century, doing endless loads of wash takes a toll on the body. Like the members of the Washing Society, today's laundry workers put a tremendous amount of effort and care into their work: they believe that "every fold matters," a phrase that resonates throughout the project.

The story, as revealed by historian Tera Hunter in her book *To 'Joy My Freedom: Southern Black Women's Lives and Labors after the Civil War,* of how the Atlanta Washing Society of 1881 won its campaign for higher wages and professional recognition, makes clear the impact of community building and solidarity. But it is not the beginning nor the end of African American women's fight to be recognized as workers with the autonomy to negotiate hours and pay. The Washing Society was organized just two decades after the end of enslavement. Some of its members had been born into the enslavement system and others were born to mothers who had been enslaved. Even before they began to organize for better wages, they had already transformed the conditions of their labor by becoming independent contractors. The film introduces their aspirations and demands as well as their mistreatment at the hands of those who rely on them for clean clothes and fresh sheets. What it doesn't show is that simply being able to work outside the confines of "the master's house" required determination and struggle, laying the foundation for the laundresses' later citywide strike.

Following the Civil War, Southerners of what had been the "master" class wanted to recreate the antebellum hierarchy to any degree possible, given that they no longer had complete control over those who worked for them. Freed people, they imagined, would perform the same tasks as they had before Emancipation, in the same houses and on the same land, for close to no pay. But for Black women, freedom was not compatible with a return to the indignities, denigrations, violence, and sexual assaults they faced when trapped inside white people's homes. They wanted to run their own households and care for their own families and wage work had to fit into and support this new autonomy. The grueling labor described in The Washing Society's first moments—making washtubs from beer barrels, soap from lye, and starch from wheat bran; carrying gallons of water from wells, pumps, or hydrants; building fires to boil the water; scrubbing, boiling, and rinsing the clothes; hanging the clothes to dry; smoothing the wrinkles with hot hand irons; lugging the heavy loads back and forth from their homes to their clients—was preferable to being at the mercy of a single employer. Working out of their own homes or in public open spaces, the women could organize their days as they saw fit, and were able to keep their children with them as they worked.

But white employers still thought they were entitled to Black women's labor, paying them next to nothing: the founders of the Washing Society each received a total of one to two dollars a week, from all their clients combined. White Southerners still did not believe that African American women had the right to offer or withhold their labor, and it took going on strike to prove that their labor was no longer available simply on demand. The laundresses were seeking a reasonable rate of pay, but just as important was the implicit demand that they be recognized as workers and citizens with the right to self-determination. They were seeking recognition, respect, and dignity. The strike's success was based on the fact that the availability of clean clothes and linens was taken for granted. Their customers could not imagine that the daughters of the enslaved had any choice but to continue doing their wash for a pittance. They had to be proven wrong.

Despite the success of the Washing Society, African American women and other women of color have continued to dominate the overworked and underpaid service sector of our economy. Throughout the Jim Crow era, white Southerners' ability to hire Black women and girls to clean their houses and do their laundry was not only a convenience, but was also a status marker. To maintain and publicize their place in a racial hierarchy based on white supremacy, even working-class and poor whites found it worthwhile to scrape together enough small change to pay school-age Black girls to help with their housework. In the North, during the Great Depression, unemployed Black women would gather on street corners where, as NAACP organizer Ella Baker and radical journalist Marvel Cooke wrote in 1935, "The lower middle-class housewife, who, having dreamed of the luxury of a maid, found opportunity staring her in the face in the form of Negro women pressed to the wall by poverty, starvation and discrimination."[1] The gathering places where potential employers would walk up and down the line of available workers, closely scrutinizing the women they might hire, were colloquially known as "slave markets." The housewives offered ten cents an hour or a dollar a day and frequently found excuses to not pay what they had promised.

Even as laundry work was industrialized to serve institutional customers like hotels and hospitals, the pattern continued. Actor Jasmine Holloway becomes the link between past and present. She reappears in another of the film's scenes, wearing her own clothes instead of the floor-length white dress that transformed her into a member of the nineteenth-century Washing Society. Sitting beside her is her actual grandmother Lula who, it turns out, had done the assembly line version of laundry work (washing on one floor, drying on another, folding on another) from 1968 to 1999. Even though Lula and her colleagues belonged to a union, they could go for weeks without getting paid and somehow it was assumed that they would continue to show up. Recognizing that the union that was supposed to be representing them was doing nothing, the workers eventually walked out in a wildcat strike. Lula describes picketing in front of the laundry building

---

1   Ella Baker and Marvel Cooke, "The Bronx Slave Market," *The Crisis* 42, no. 10 (1935): 330–31 and 340, at 330.

and getting filmed by TV news cameras. Shortly after that, she and her coworkers got their back pay. Once again, laundry work was made visible by its absence: you can picture their labor as tables without tablecloths, beds without sheets, and bodies without clean clothing.

The desire to be treated with dignity and respect animates today's laundry workers just as it did the members of the Washing Society and Lula Holloway. African American workers' terms of employment shifted from "bondage to contract," to use historian Amy Dru Stanley's phrase.[2] They had to fight not only for wages, but to be recognized as the owners of their bodies and labor. Immigrant workers, especially the undocumented, those who are not white, and those not fluent in English, have also had their work undervalued and their humanity ignored by the very people who rely on them for the essential service they provide. "Because you work in a laundromat, people think you are lesser than them," Margarita Lopez explains. She experiences racism as a Latina and is sometimes assumed to be undocumented. "Lesser than" is about the intersection of race and class, but it is also about the fact that service work is seen as "unskilled" labor — something anyone can do. In the past, service work was done by people from whom subservience was expected and who were not paid for their time and effort: the enslaved, on the one hand, and wives and daughters on the other.

Although *The Washing Society* was made two years before the COVID-19 lockdown, it is especially poignant to watch in its aftermath. The pandemic forced us to acknowledge that the least glamorous work is often the most essential to sustaining life and health, but did not require us to reward or care for those essential workers in substantive ways. Those with means relied on people who had no other choice to do their shopping and other errands, protecting themselves while putting others at risk. In an economic landscape where fewer households have a member whose time is exclusively devoted to domestic labor, we rely on laundry workers to free customers' time for "more important things" — their professional jobs, their family time, their leisure, and self-care. While not the visible status symbol of a household employee (a visitor to one's home sees no evidence of who does the wash), the perception that one person's time is more valuable than another's ("I have better things to do with my time than someone who has to work in a laundromat") leads to a sense of social as well as economic superiority ("If my time is more valuable, I must be more important"). But these workers do not live to serve; they provide services to make a living. They, too, need "family time" and "leisure time." Higher wages are necessary to make that possible, but so is the recognition that they are not just hands putting quarters into washing machines and folding the clothes they take out. They are the other side of what should be a fair exchange of labor for payment that also includes a "hello" or "good morning."

---

2   Amy Dru Stanley, *From Bondage to Contract: Wage Labor, Marriage, and the Market in the Age of Slave Emancipation* (Cambridge: Cambridge University Press, 1998).

Reflections on Laundry and Reproductive Labor: In Conversation with Silvia Federici

Since 2021, we've been visiting with Silvia Federici in her Brooklyn apartment, drinking her marvelous Italian coffee, and helping her to organize her paper archive of research and writing. In between sorting and filing her materials on witch hunts, capital punishment, student activism in Africa, and reproductive labor, we've had the profound experience of being in conversation with Silvia. In this conversation, we asked Silvia to discuss how she and fellow feminist activists in the 1970s Wages for Housework movement fought for domestic work as wage labor within a capitalist economy.

Lizzie: *Let's talk about the work you did in New York City organizing with Wages for Housework. We know that laundromats were one of the first places where you handed out pamphlets and provided information to women.*

Silvia Federici: This was, for us, one of the main spaces where you could meet a lot of women. Since they were involved in doing the reproductive work, in doing housework, they would be particularly open to listening, and also would be there together, collectively. I remember there would be ten to fifteen women sitting there for an hour waiting for their clothes to wash or to dry. They'd be washing the clothes and having to entertain their children. So, we could go in and give out flyers and engage in a conversation. Historically, women never did the laundry alone. The laundromat as a place was, in a sense, the last embodiment of a long history of women working together in one space. Putting a price on this work was the most effective way for the Wages for Housework campaign to convey this point.

When I was growing up in Italy during the war, the women would bring their wooden tubs to the village square, and they would do the laundry together. It was a place for... how do you say, a sharing and circulation of

WAGES FOR HOUSEWORK

NOTICE TO ALL GOVERNMENTS

The women of the world are serving notice. We clean your homes and factories. We raise the next generation of workers for you. Whatever else we may do, we are the housewives of the world. In return for our work, you have only asked us to work harder.

We are serving notice to you that we intend to be paid for the work we do. We want wages for every dirty toilet, every painful childbirth, every indecent assault, every cup of coffee and every smile. And if we don't get what we want, then we will simply refuse to work any longer.

We have brought our children to be good citizens and to respect your laws and you have put them in factories, in prisons, in ghettos and in typing pools. Our children deserve more than you can offer and now we will bring them up to EXPECT more.

We have borne babies for you when you needed more workers, and we have submitted to sterilization when you didn't. Our wombs are not government property any longer.

We have scrubbed and polished and oiled and waxed and scoured until our arms and backs ached, and you have only created more dirt. Now you will rot in your own garbage.

We have worked in the isolation of our homes when you needed us to and we have taken on a second job too when you needed that. Now we want to decide WHEN we work, HOW we work, and WHO we work for. We want to be able to decide NOT TO WORK AT ALL --like you.

We are teachers and nurses and secretaries and prostitutes and actresses and childcare workers and hostesses and waitresses and cooks and cleaning ladies and workers of every variety. We have sweated while you have grown rich. Now we want back the wealth we have produced. WE WANT IT IN CASH, RETROACTIVE AND IMMEDIATELY. AND WE WANT ALL OF IT.

THE CAMPAIGN FOR WAGES FOR HOUSEWORK

knowledge and experience. They would learn from each other, feel connected and develop a viewpoint.

You could still see this in laundromats, when the women pull out their pants and shirts, and so on. Immediately, there will be conversation because there is a story attached to any one of those garments. But, over the last few decades, there's been an incorporation of the washing machine into the home, which in a way is more convenient, but in another way, also intensifies the isolation of women. There is a fragmentation of the process of reproduction and the community collectivity that women have shared historically. So, today, it would not be as easy to carry on the kind of organizing we were doing with Wages for Housework in the 1970s.

Lynne: *What did your flyers say back then?*

Silvia: They said this is the work that most women do that keeps the world going and when the next meeting would be. In 1975, we opened up a small gathering space with a big store window on Eighth Street and Fifth Avenue in Brooklyn. The door was always open when we were there. Women could just walk in.

Thinking about this, I'm reminded of a movie that I saw in the '70s, *Clotheslines* by Roberta Cantow. In the film, Cantow sees clotheslines as a form of art. Women don't just hang the clothes, but they have a whole strategy with the pants, the socks, a whole construction, right? It's very beautiful—with the colors, the shapes and the ordering. There's an imaginative ordering that follows a logic. It seems to me that Cantow is offering a reevaluation of reproductive work, a reevaluation of domestic work that is generally very devalued if not almost despised, right?

Lizzie: *Yes, Cantow's film explores doing laundry from such an original perspective, celebrating its creativity. You've also talked about laundry as a form of reproductive labor with an economic value.*

Silvia: Women are reproducing the workforce, and reproducing it with a tremendous amount of energy and intelligence. This work is not recognized and has been made invisible. The Wages for Housework campaign was precisely that, a refusal of invisibility. This work is not a personal service. It's not something women do because it's our human nature. It's work that is part of the organization of labor that is socially constructed from the point of view of a capitalist economy that exploits the energy of a whole population. So, this is the reproduction of people's capacity to work. In the end, reproductive domestic labor is not something that solely benefits the family. It also benefits society at large, particularly for the employers of the wage earners who are being supported at home, you know?

Domestic work is a form of capitalist production. It is part of the great assembly line that is, in fact, the reproduction of the workforce, but not goods for the market. There is rarely substantial remuneration, benefits, or a pension. It's a scandal, but this is the logic of capitalism.

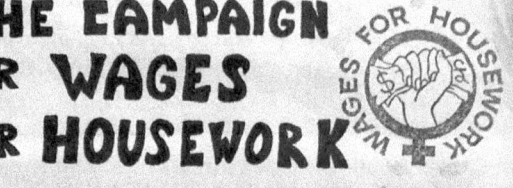

THE CAMPAIGN FOR WAGES FOR HOUSEWORK

LOVE DOESN'T PAY THE BILLS

MONEY IS CHOICE

The New York WAGES FOR HOUSEWORK COMMITTEE is part of a nationwide organization that is campaigning for WAGES FOR HOUSEWORK from the government for

ALL WOMEN

married or not — with or without children — with or without a second job
native or immigrant — lesbian or straight

HOUSEWORK IS OUR COMMON PROBLEM
LET'S MAKE IT OUR COMMON STRUGGLE

We demand WAGES FOR HOUSEWORK because we cannot afford to work endless hours in the home and then depend on a man or on welfare or have to take a second job BECAUSE WE HAVE NO MONEY we can call our own. Nobody works as much as we do. WE ALL NEED MORE MONEY NOT MORE WORK.

WE'RE NEVER UNEMPLOYED WE'RE JUST UNPAID

Business and Government profit from our work — THEY SHOULD PAY FOR IT. We know they need us so we can set the terms.

WE DEMAND **WAGES FOR HOUSEWORK**

- To cut down on housework — to eat out, get machines to do some of the work, and refuse to be slaves to the house

WE HAVE SACRIFICED ENOUGH OF OUR LIVES

- To be able to decide working conditions and wages on the second job, and *if* we want it in the first place
- To stand up to men when we work WITH them and when we work FOR them — if we had our own money we could
- To decide what our sex lives should be like
- To decide if, when and under what conditions to have children
- To give our children what we want them to have
- To demand and WIN paid holidays away from ALL work
- To demand and WIN decent housing

JOIN OUR CAMPAIGN

All over the US and in several other countries of the world women are organizing speak outs, rallies, marches for WAGES FOR HOUSEWORK. We speak in different languages but we are all saying the same thing.

WE ARE OPENING **OUR CAMPAIGN OFFICE** IN A STOREFRONT
288 B 8th Street (off 5th Ave) in BROOKLYN
Come and visit us while shopping

WEDNESDAYS and SATURDAYS 11 a.m. to 4 p.m. tel. 965 4112
New York WAGES FOR HOUSEWORK COMMITTEE — We have discussion groups, video tapes, cassettes, literature, speakers available to talk with your group. (Non-office hours call : 788 2822)

Essentially, capitalism presents itself as a democratic system, a system based on an equal exchange, but actually, it's really based on different forms of enslavement, different forms of unpaid work. This is what allows for the accumulation of wealth in a colonial society, whether historically through enslavement, which never finished, or domestic labor.

Today, we see growth in the global economy that has actually led to a massive expansion of the informal, underpaid labor force. The logic of capitalism is to pay workers less and less. The whole issue of housework, domestic work, reproduction—the whole panoply of feminist issues—gives us a real window into this arrangement.

I can speak for myself. I didn't want to have to do any housework. By the time I was fifteen, I said, I don't want to marry. I'm not going to have children. I don't want to do any of this. I'd seen my mother. I didn't want to repeat my mother's life.

Much of what makes the work oppressive is precisely the miserable conditions. It's been organized in a way that isolates us from each other, which I think is a political decision, you know, because, in this way, the isolation, this move toward more and more private space, it's really a way of weakening the possibility of collective resistance.

Lynne: *Could you take yourself back to a moment when you walked into a laundromat with the idea of organizing?*

Silvia: When we were going into laundromats then, it was like entering a big kitchen. You would see children running all about. And there would be all this energy around the different stages of laundry: the folding and the switching from machine to the dryer, the putting away of the clothes. The sociality was so important. There was always a conversation going on. In looking at the politics of women's consciousness and reflecting on it, this made for a very charged space.

I think that when you go back, you know, particularly to the 1970s, you're talking about a time in which the sexual division of labor was much more pronounced. Not that the laundromat is less of a female space now, but women who in 1974-75 may have been in the laundromat would probably have a job outside the home now.

Lizzie: *Where does paid laundry work, dropping off your clothes for others to clean, fit into all of this?*

Silvia: Our whole history of reproductive work will be written by looking at the history of laundry. Most people now look at the experience that I was talking about as a waste of time. Nobody wants to sit and wait for their clothes to be washed and dried. So, the more efficient way of doing it is to leave the bag and pick it up later, or do it in your own machine.

There is less time for children, less time for the elderly, less time for those who are sick, and less time also for the kind of activities where a woman might sit for an hour waiting for the wash cycle to finish with other women in a common space. All of this appears as progress, because now

you may have a washing machine in your own apartment, and you may have a job outside the home. But is something being lost in terms of a collective experience?

And yet, the actors in your film *The Washing Society* communicate a mixture of rebellion and resignation. They portray laundromat workers who've experienced a lifetime of condemnation. They show us that the work is so repetitive, you know, terrible when you're sentenced to do the same movement, the same thing, all day, for hours and hours.

So even though it appears to be less exploitive because it is paid, in fact it's worse in some ways, right? First of all, the pay is minimal, and clearly, there is a connection between low wages and the fact that women do it. Most people who do laundry work are immigrant women of color.

There's a connection between what happens in the home and what happens outside the home. There's a profound link between how women have been doing domestic work for nothing and its massive social devaluation. When the work goes out of the home, it becomes, in fact, an extension of that devaluation. Somebody's doing that work, and under what conditions are they doing the work?

Lynne: *These are some of the reasons that so few of the people who work in the laundromats were willing to be interviewed on camera.*

Silvia: I mean, there's been raids upon raids upon raids of "undocumented" workers in New York, you know, with people being arrested and deported, taken to the airport directly. Not even being allowed to go home and tell their children. I mean, the cruelty, the barbarity of the system.... There's a big movement in the nation right now, of domestic workers. It's really powerful. So, I think the next one will be a movement of laundry workers.

Lizzie: *Visualizing lint was an important aspect of our film. What does the lint evoke for you when you see that material that comes out of the dryers?*

Silvia: Detergents, dealing with all that—the machines, the heat, the boiling water, and chemicals. The unhealthy environment that these workers are in all through the day. Also, having to stand so much of the day. You know, probably developing varicose veins while they are folding and folding and folding.

Some years ago, in France, I think, they did a study of thousands of workers, and they discovered that their dreams were deeply influenced by their daily work activities. I was thinking of the dreams of these women—these things that you want to throw away, like lint.

Daily life is full of entropy. Things fall apart continuously, and things get dirty, and things get messy. Now people have their nice, beautiful, clean things, but meanwhile, there are the workers who have touched all those germs. They have been breathing those invisible chemicals. What's visible is the nice package. Poof, you drop it and you get it back clean. Capitalism is a happy system. You can pay a little bit, and you can get your stuff done, but the danger to people's health, both physical and psychological—that's kept behind the scenes.

HAND BOOK

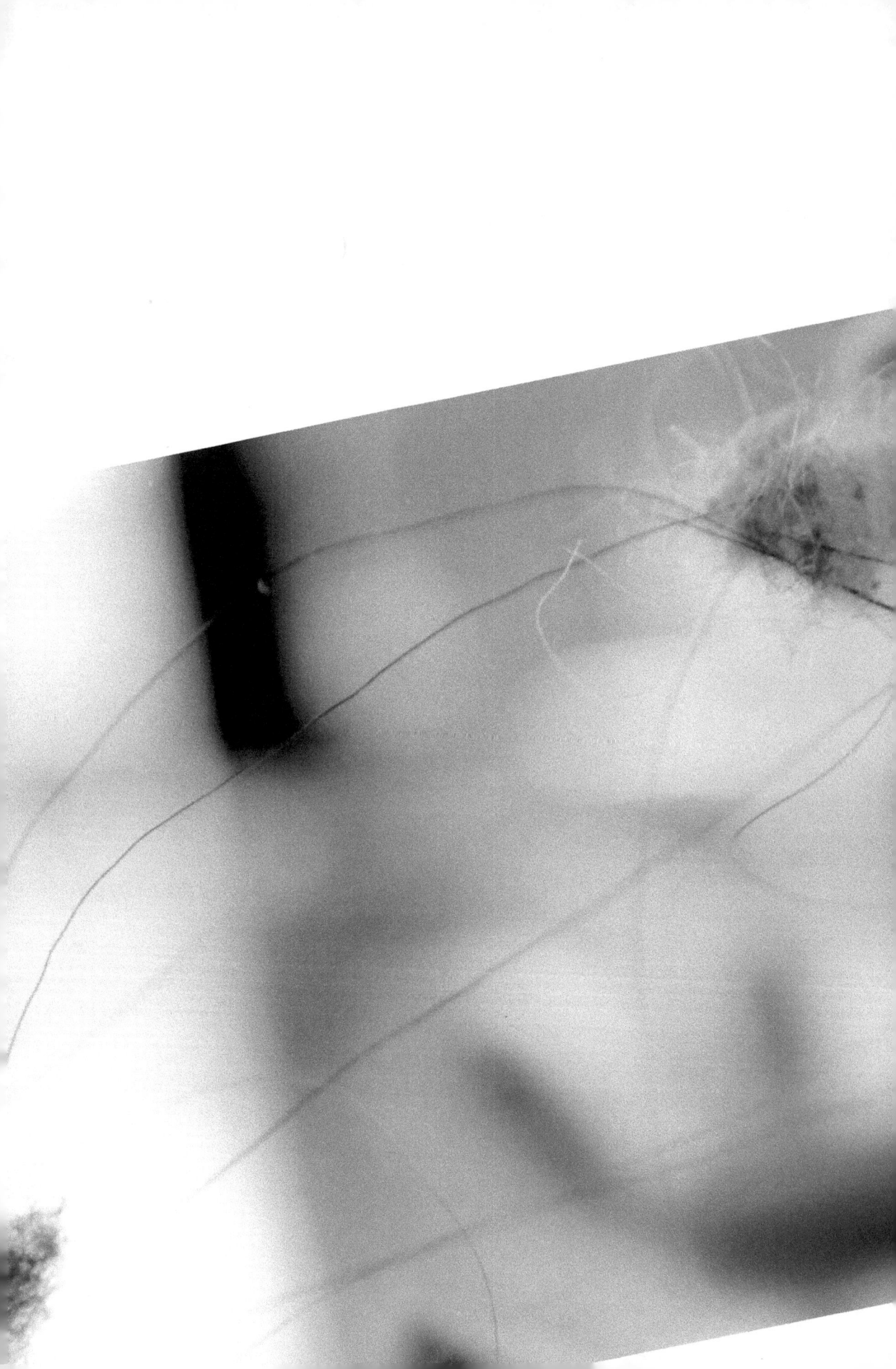

AID

Lizzie Olesker

I was spending more and more time taking care of my mother. She was in her late eighties and living alone in an apartment that she'd waited over ten years to get through a program for moderate-income seniors. It had a small, sooty balcony at the back where she "planted" plastic red and pink roses that were always in bloom. She started to have a hard time walking by herself. She would lose her balance while crossing the street and was having trouble stepping onto the curb at each corner. Suddenly, she wasn't able to get in or out of a taxi on her own and would ask the cab driver or some other random passing person if they could help her. My mother told me that she would sometimes just be frozen with fear and would stand there on the street, holding on to a lamppost, yelling out to anyone who could hear her—to some young man who happened to walk by—she would call out to them, "Excuse me! Excuse me, can you come over here and help me?" And they would, which amazed me. I went over to her apartment as often as I could, would shop at the grocery store, take her to her exercise class, and then head to rehearsal….

I finally had to hire someone to come help but could only afford to pay for a few hours at a time. It felt like when I'd had young children and you had to be with them all the time, take care of them and just watch them, and how your hands were sore and stiff from holding them tightly and telling them everything would be okay. It was what you did because you loved them but also because you had to because there was no one else to do it.

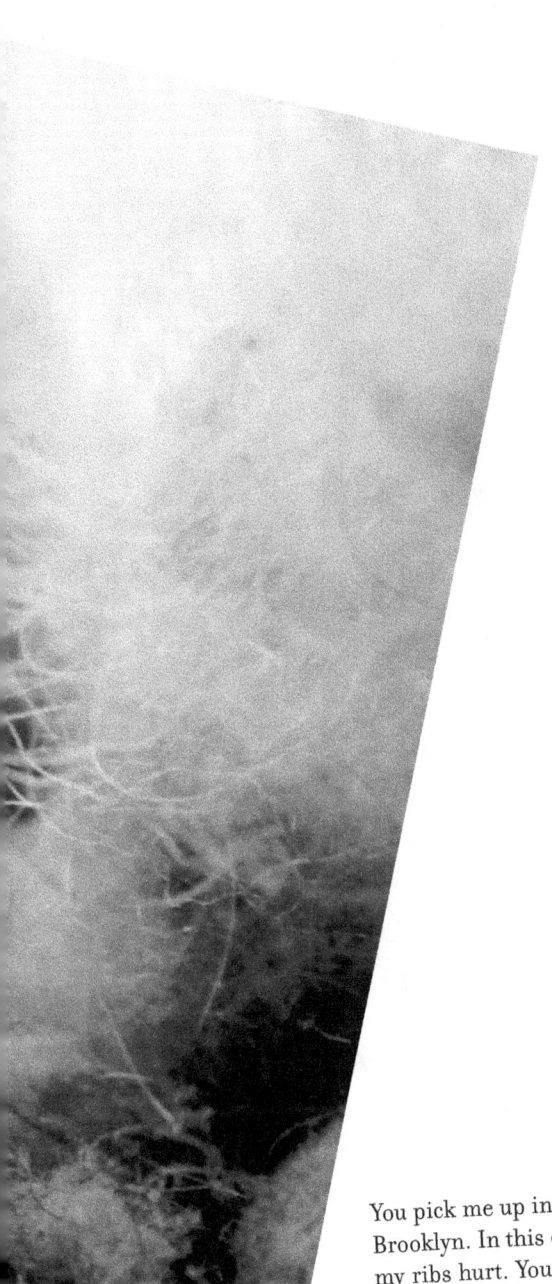

worry

Lynne Sachs

You pick me up in a grey Toyota and we begin our drive to an interview in Brooklyn. In this closed quiet space, I tell you about my cough that makes my ribs hurt. You tell me about blood on your underwear when blood on our underwear stopped long ago. I tell you about my dying grandmother and how the closer to death she gets, the meaner she becomes. You tell me about your fears that your son might not graduate. You tell me about long days with your charming mother, holding on to her presence before her final goodbye. I recount my fear of finishing a film about my father that may reveal more than I want to share. You tell me I must. After all the joys of writing our play, we finish it and don't know how to let it go. I worry that my daughters don't feel good about who they are. You worry that your son's passions may lead him down a path you don't understand. We stop at the place where our work will begin, and I know we have arrived.

QUESTIONS ON BLACK AND WHITE: A PHOTOGRAPH BY GERTRUDE KASEBIER

We were looking for archival images of women washing.
We had researched the Atlanta washerwomen's strike of 1881.
There were no photos of that strike —

Not in the Archive.
Nothing, in terms of images.
We've been told they don't exist.

I was looking for some kind of visual documentation.

I accidentally came across a photo that I could not ignore when I looked up "19th-century laundress" on the Internet.
This image came up.
There she was.
Everywhere, at least when you were looking for her.

Unlike the washerwomen of 1881, you found *her*
in a lot of places.

I threw the image file into Google Images and found another caption with a little more information: *"Black and White: an informal portrait of a young negro woman surrounded by laundry in Newport, Rhode Island."*

To me, it looks like it was taken with one of those large-format cameras and a tripod.

The photographer was clearly a professional, or at least someone who works in that way.

That's what I imagine.

HAND BOOK

When I look at it closely, I feel the energy of the "moment." The passage of time.
I'm aware of the wind. Motion. Stillness.

The wind is important.
Even the sheet seems like it's moving.
Look at the blur of the black stockings.

Photographs are taken. The subject is captured.
Framed.

This one's owned by Getty Images and was taken by a woman named Gertrude Kasebier.
(How do you pronounce her name?)

(I have no idea.)

I just looked up Kasebier. She's referred to as a *pictorialist*.
What does that imply exactly?
Who was Kasebier in relationship to the woman in the image, the photo's *subject?*

I can't find anything about her, the laundress, not even her name.

That's not surprising.

There's plenty about Gertrude Kasebier, though. She produced many mother-daughter portraits, typical of the early 20th Century. They have an idealized, fuzzy, and dreamy look to them.

From what I've read, Kasebier had a complicated relationship to motherhood—and marriage. She was very ambitious and wanted to earn a living as a professional photographer. Even though her husband set her up with a commercial photography studio, she still felt pressure to sell her work.

The images look like Impressionist paintings, very Renoir. They make motherhood look comforting and uncomplicated.

They're all posing—in a way that fulfills societal expectations at that time.

In the so-called *fin de siècle*.

Kasebier did gain some recognition with her portraits of Native Americans, called "Show Indians." Alfred Stieglitz was impressed by those portraits.

There's a kind of violation happening here where they're extricated from their actual lives and put into this alien, commercial environment.

Objectified—

Modified—

Exoticized.

Yes, that's what she was doing.

It's ambiguous —

I don't know—

Well, I think the "Show Indians" were photographed by Kasebier in a formal, seemingly respectful way.

Yes, but they're also being objectified.

But there is a kind of dignity and gravity to the images, and a solemnity. We're seeing them performing themselves.

They're acting. They're pretending. They're not just being.

Yes, they are just *being* but in a conscious way. As soon as you turn the camera on a person, they're performing for you, in some sense. That's something we wanted to examine in our film.

Let's go back to Kasebier's photograph, also called "Woman Doing Laundry." It was taken just a few decades after Reconstruction, during the state-sanctioned trauma of Jim Crow.

It is a picture of a Black woman providing a service. She's not hanging laundry for herself. But I could be wrong.

Gertrude Kasebier is behind the camera. We are also white women holding the camera...

... at or toward our subjects.

The "Woman Doing Laundry" is posing for the camera and performing. The photograph may seem to have a kind of dignity, but at the same time the question arises: for whom?

For whom is she performing? Why is she smiling?

What year was it?

1902.

That's over 120 years ago, and there she is. The camera seems to have caught her in the middle of working. She's literally bending down to take another sheet to put on the clothesline.

She's being interrupted.

Are we looking at a staged moment or a so-called actual moment, a documentary event?

There's this gaze between the woman in the image and the photographer, Gertrude.

I think the woman in the photo makes us aware of our own voyeurism.

Even our exploitation.

She says:

I dare you to think about me.
I dare you to synthesize me into your art.
I dare you to look back at me and to actually think about who you are

in relationship to me.

Loads of Prose: From the Beginning

Emily Rubin

> *I enjoy a venue where you are reading to the not already converted.*
> — Marie Ponsot, poet[1]

> *A "happening" is all about having a group of people interact with their environment. Happenings invite us to cast aside for a moment these proper manners and partake wholly in the real nature of the art and life. It is a rough and sudden act, where one often feels 'dirty,' and dirt, we might begin to realize, is also organic and fertile, and everything including the visitors can grow a little into such circumstances.*
> — Allan Kaprow, artist[2]

Venues in my neighborhood were closing in the rush of the real estate highs of the early 2000s. Drugs were briefly waning and spaces for experimentation were shuttered: sold or rented for premium prices. The laundromat was a percussive thought that came over us as my friend and I sipped beers at a bar on Avenue C in the Lower East Side of New York City.

Down a few blocks was the laundromat where I had been a patron for years. I would walk from my building past people waiting at bus stops and Watchtower acolytes with brochures in front of a temple with no windows. I carried my loads into the dry, soap-scented air to the waiting machines. The woman who did the washing and folding smiled with gold-filled teeth and was precise about every fold. I thought about what other things might happen in this space at night while TVs orbiting overhead brought talking-heads delivering news and telenovelas from the world outside. It was here at the Avenue C Laundromat that the first Loads of Prose event would take place.

I invited two author friends to read their work among the washers and dryers on a late Saturday night. The fluorescent lights buzzed over a hand-

---

[1] Personal communication.
[2] Allen Kaprow, "Happenings in the New York Scene" (1961), in *Essays on the Blurring of Art and Life,* ed. Jeff Kelley (Berkeley: University of California Press, 2003), 18.

ful of people still doing laundry. One of the writers looked at me, his eyes squinted, as he gazed upon the narrow aisles and said, "Why do a reading in a laundromat?"

I gently asked the proprietor if the TVs could be silenced during the reading. "Okay," he said with a nod and a flick of a cigarette to the curb.

The writers took center stage in cycles of quarter-timed rhythms while the neighborhood customers and night staff continued to wash and fold, reminding us that stories float alongside, above, and below. I tapped the microphone to alert the crowd and passed around a laundry bag for donations. A radio journalist arrived after covering a story of a coyote loose in Central Park to find out what this laundromat reading was all about.

Above the sloshing clothes, stories were spoken, broadcast over a borrowed mic and amp. We listened closely, slowing down, folding into each other around the warmth and rumble, absorbing what we heard from start to finish. Intimate stories were revealed, like pockets turned inside out. The machine doors opened, rattling and revealing motes, threads, and leftover pilling. It was over in an hour. We said "thank you" and "goodbye" to the proprietor.

Back on the street, the moon shadows of two-story high ginkgo trees tattooed the sidewalk. We scanned the sides of buildings up to the rooftops lit by stars, streetlights, and low-flying helicopter searchlights. Through the laundromat windows, we saw the TVs go back on, the images return. On that sultry hot night, Avenue C carried us home, our carts filled with washed clothes and pages shuffled into newly ordered arrangements.

Since that first evening at Avenue C and 5th Street, there have been more than eighty readings in working laundromats around the country, from New York City to San Francisco, Boulder, and Stockbridge. Altogether, more than 120 writers and musicians have shared their words and music with local audiences.

I invited Lizzie Olesker and Lynne Sachs to create a piece for performance for the Loads of Prose series. Over many months, I then helped search for a laundromat willing to take a risk and present a site-specific production in their storefront space. I found the New Lucky Laundromat in the Clinton Hill area of Brooklyn. Cautiously, the owner agreed to let us present our hybrid performance *Every Fold Matters*. For three frigid February nights, the cast performed to a full audience in coats, hats, and gloves, sitting on top of machines and in metal folding chairs, after the last wash.

Reception Theory

A "text" — be it a book, movie, or other creative work — is not simply passively accepted by the audience, but the reader/viewer interprets the meanings of the text based on her or his individual cultural background and life experiences. In essence, the meaning of a text is not inherent within the text itself, but is created within the relationship between the text and the reader.
— Stuart Hall, "Encoding and Decoding in the Television Discourse"[1]

Performance is not a one-way communication. It's a dialogue with an audience that engages in a complex interactive thought process in response to what they're seeing and hearing. Cultural theorist Stuart Hall suggests that media contains a variety of encoded messages that are then decoded by audiences. People are silent during a theatrical performance or film: this is the behavioral convention. How might we have access to our audience's interpretations? We felt it was important to have this, so we invited audience members to speak or write their thoughts. Here we share a selection of varied and revealing responses to our live performance *Every Fold Matters* and to our film *The Washing Society*.

* * *

Just a note after the performance at the New Lucky Laundromat. The multilayered intersections of film and performance, documentary and fiction, reality and imagination, employee and customer, historical fact and personal anecdote, not to mention the mix and drama of local "characters" in a laundromat setting (you could not have asked for a better "set" — each weathered sign on the wall, each old-fashioned washer/dryer, all of the fluorescent lights, etc.) — added rich flavor and texture to the work. You made us rethink the laundromat as a site of urban convergence, where strangers of different races, religions, languages, and classes make ritualistic visits to a public space that's also

---

[1] Stuart Hall, "Encoding and Decoding in the Television Discourse" (1973), in *Writings on Media*, eds. Stuart Hall and Charlotte Brunsdon (Durham: Duke University Press, 2021), 247–66.

The Workers Unite Film Festival Presents

EVERY FOLD MATTERS

a live performance with film
by Lizzie Olesker & Lynne Sachs
with Jasmine Holloway, Veraalba Santa, Tony Torn & Ching Valdes-Aran

May 5, 7:00pm
The Tank - 151 W 46th st, NYC

May 13, 14 & 16, 8pm
May 15, 3pm
Union Docs - 322 Union Ave, Brooklyn

$15/$12 (students & seniors)

workersunitefilmfestival.org
everyfoldmatters.com

a functional extension of their own homes, and play out their needs, moods, and assorted psychopathologies with one another (for better or for worse), one quarter at a time; a place where people try to remove their stains, their strains, and their secrets.

— Alan Berliner, filmmaker

I've been struggling with dance lately. The more trained the dancer, the more singularly categorized the dancing is, the less focused I can stay. The less trained, more everyday movement is what interests me. And I felt that the movement in the piece was just that — everyday, and thus more compelling. Best of all was how the three women interacted with the clothes which became characters in their hands.

— Kathy O'Dell, art historian, critic, and Associate Professor Emerita, University of Maryland, Baltimore County

I was thinking about the performance *Every Fold Matters* and how it reframes the power relations and authority that run within cities and public spaces and within image making, language, and representation. We saw this explicitly in the non-subtitling of the Chinese and Spanish sequences, but also in the way the piece de-authorized knowledge, for example, by having folks recite lines from memory, and then read from scripts — asking us to think about whose knowledge or words were these? The live performers reference themselves on film, and later their silhouettes speak, so we see real people in contrast to mediated ones. The end result seems to be an experiment on de-centering the authority of images and words.

— Chi-hui Yang, film scholar and Senior Program Officer, Ford Foundation

When the worker pockets the hundred-dollar bills — as a viewer, at that moment, I started watching with a different intensity. I felt the piece sharpen from a broader social context into a specific dramatic moment that I knew would have narrative repercussions down the line. I asked myself questions about these workers' conditions, along with formal and reflexive questions about what you've gained or lost by choosing this unusual mode of documentation.

— Pacho Velez, filmmaker

This performance builds the image of Asian immigrant workers. I feel the intimacy with the characters. The performance does not portray the immigrant workers as isolated strangers who come from another world. Even though I've never worked in a laundromat, I connect with the workers who have to finish their tedious and difficult jobs. In the past, I have seen many projects portray Asian immigrants in an old-school anthropologist's style. I don't like the way that those projects interpret and analyze immigrants' behaviors, where Asian immigrants are treated as "the other" and audiences are encouraged to show sympathy for the weak "other."

— Lingyun Zheng, filmmaker

Bringing in a Chinese translator allowed Olesker and Sachs new levels of access at some laundromats, establishing trust and eliciting stories. But it still wasn't enough to get more than a handful of laundry workers to be recorded. The majority of the workers were tight-lipped. Whether for fear of repercussions from management, mistrust of how their stories would be used, or reticence as a code of conduct, the reluctance was so widespread it was itself indicative of something about the job. This spirit of refusal is wound throughout the piece in recurring sequences of chaos, in which the denials are spoken simultaneously by multiple actors, in three languages; one doesn't need a translator to understand they're saying no.
— Ginny Mohler, "Laundromat-Theater: Where Every Fold Matters," *The Brooklyn Rail*, February, 2015

The ghost of the Washing Society provides a historical context for the piece, balancing it against the absurd, often cruel, altercations which take place inside the present-day laundromat. The legacy of domestic work, the issues surrounding power, and the exchange of money for services are all potent themes that rise to the surface and bubble over in dramatic, thrilling escalations of the everyday. A laundromat is a public space where something private occurs; it is the opposite of a typical theater, a private space in which a public event occurs. Nearly every element of *Every Fold Matters* pushes the boundaries of what is private and what is public, what is real and what is fiction, and where we find narrative fulfillment in any of the above.
— Michelle Chen, "Laundromat Workers Air New York's Dirty Laundry in Performance Piece," *In These Times*, July, 2015

i wonder if the people you spoke with for the film ever talked about what repetition makes possible? often, repetition — when discussed in terms of certain kinds of labor — is talked about as having a negative impact on the thought and imagination of the worker. but in music, repetition is often considered to be a practice that allows for the flourishing of deeply meditative, contemplative thought to emerge. so my question was if the women ever talked about repetition as producing a capacity for thought experience they'd not otherwise have? this is not to celebrate conditions of poverty or exploitation in the political economy but to ask what poverty and exploitation of the political economy continue to fail to destroy. because what it fails to destroy is a gift.
— ashon crawley, author and Professor of Religious Studies and African American and African Studies, University of Virginia

I bring a Marxist perspective to the interviews with the workers in the film *The Washing Society*. I was thinking about Jean Rouch's interviews with factory workers in Paris in his 1961 film *Chronicle of a Summer*. In the film, the anthropologist Edgar Morin interviews a Renault factory worker who explains his condition of exploitation and the reproduction of his labor that is necessary to be able to work the next day. He says, "I

feel like I work 24 hours. I have a 9-hour shift and the rest of the time, I'm sleeping to work" (rough translation), which means that for the revival of his labor, he needs to eat, sleep, and take care of himself, thus replenishing his ability to work for his boss the next day. One can say, there is also the unpaid reproductive labor of women in the home that traditionally has provided this nourishment to male laborers, in addition to providing for the new generation of laborers who will enter the workforce. In Marxist theory, this can be understood as "the production of labor-power [which] consists of [the individual's] reproduction of themselves or his maintenance." Feminist scholar Silvia Federici discusses this critique of the reproduction of labor-power as it relates to women in detail. The point is—as it relates to *The Washing Society*—I felt like Mr. Ho, a laundromat worker, describes his workday and daily routine (being out of the house by 7:00am, working until 7:30pm, to then do it all again the next day). He doesn't express the deeper proletariat consciousness of his hours of reproduction, which, in contrast, can be heard in the Renault factory worker's response in *Chronicle of a Summer*. Does Ho say that he eats and replenishes himself to be able to work the next day ("the reproduction of himself or his maintenance")? I'd need to watch the film again to see. On the other hand, Margarita, another laundromat worker in the film, inches closer to acknowledging and recognizing her need to replenish herself (to tend to her herniated disc, her family), she does not quite draw attention to these non-working/reproductive hours more specifically. Or does she? This Marxist framing is an interesting way to draw attention to what the workers do not say about the reproduction of their labor-power.

—Ana Almeyda-Cohen, Latin American Literature and Cinema, Assistant Professor, Colby College

I saw *The Washing Society* at Metrograph Theater in New York City. After the film, the directors talked with feminist Marxist theorist Silvia Federici who argues that domestic labor—whether in a private home or a public space—is an invisible yet vital form of production used to sustain a capitalist system. *The Washing Society* portrays the hidden lives of laundry workers and makes the invisible visible in ways that remind me of how director Chantal Akerman looked at domestic labor in her 1975 film, *Jeanne Dielman, 23, Quai du Commerce 1080 Bruxelles*. This film portrays a housewife who engages in domestic work and ultimately sex work to support herself and her teenage son. Akerman focuses on the minutiae of Jeanne Dielman's day-to-day tasks. We watch Jeanne cook meals, wash the dishes, grocery shop, and do things often considered to be menial. While *The Washing Society* brings attention to this invisible labor by employing narrative and performance techniques, Akerman forces her audience to watch domestic labor, in real time, almost minute by minute. The invisible becomes hyper-visible, and there is a visual code that guides Jeanne Dielman's actions: folding clothes, chopping vegetables, boiling water. What sets Jeanne Dielman apart from the women in *The Washing Society* is the solitary nature of

HAND BOOK

her labor. Laundromat workers wash and fold in groups and can form unions to negotiate against their bosses, while Jeanne Dielman navigates housework on her own. In the final scene of *The Washing Society*, we see two performers as laundromat workers banging and dancing in unison on top of the machines, claiming ownership of their own labor. In a world where their customers and bosses do not see the value of their work, they make themselves visible.

— Patricia Kusumaningtyas. "The Washing Society and Jeanne Dielman: Making the Invisible Visible," December 13, 2021, patriciakusumaningtyas.com

HAND BOOK

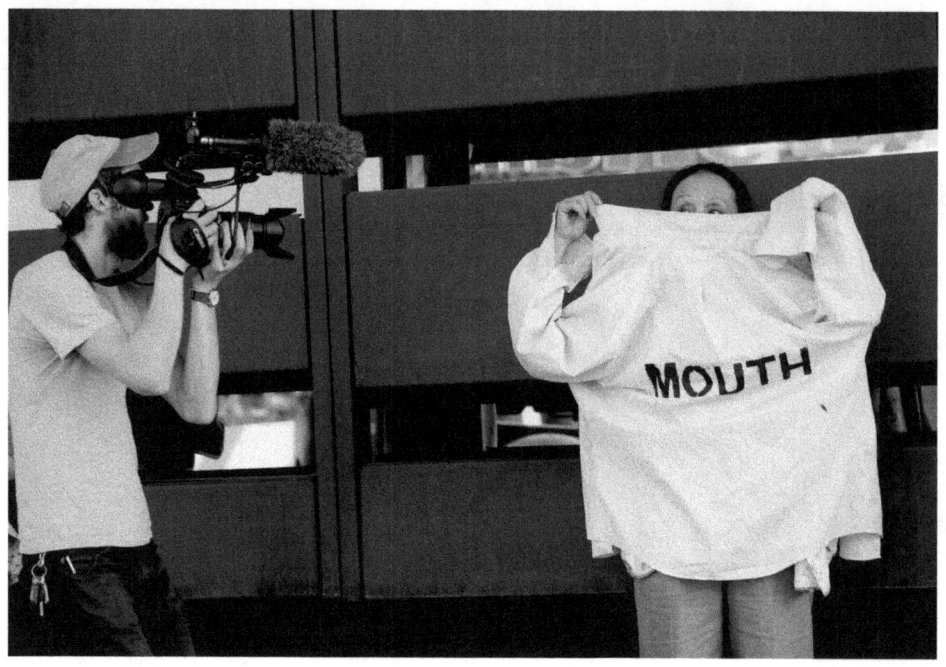

HOW IT HAPPENED: PERFORMANCES AND SCREENINGS

Every Fold Matters: Performances in New York City (2015 – 2018)

Amalgamated Lithographers Union of America, Manhattan
Asian Film Institute and Cinema Studies, New York University
Atlantis Superwash Laundromat, Brooklyn
Gentle Wash Avenue A Laundromat, East Village
Harry Van Arsdale Center for Labor Studies, SUNY, Radical Film Network
New Lucky Laundromat, Clinton Hill, Brooklyn
The Tank Performance Space, Manhattan
University Settlement, Lower East Side
UnionDocs, Workers Unite! Film Festival, Brooklyn

The Washing Society: Festivals and Other Screenings (2018 – present)

Anthology Film Archives, New York
Athens Film and Video Festival, Ohio
BAMcinemaFest, Brooklyn Academy of Music
Black Maria Film Festival, Juror's Stellar Award
Chicago Underground Film Festival
Cinema Parallels, Bosnia Herzegovina
DCTV (Downtown Community Television), New York City
Encuentros del Otro Cine Documental Festival Internacional, Ecuador
European Media Arts Festival, Osnabrück, Germany
Gene Siskel Center, Chicago
Indie Memphis, Audience Award: "Departures" (Avant-Garde)
Kinesthesia Festival, Birmingham, United Kingdom
Maine International Film Festival
Metrograph Theater, New York City
National Civil Rights Museum, Memphis
National Gallery of Art, Washington, DC
Other Cinema, San Francisco
Pacific Film Archive/Berkeley Art Museum

Queens World Film Festival, New York City
Sebastopol Documentary Film Festival
Scribe Video Center, Philadelphia
Sheffield Documentary Film Festival, United Kingdom
Vancouver International Film Festival, Canada

Selected University and College Screenings

Amherst College
Dennison College
Fashion Institute of Technology
University of Mississippi Center for the Study of Southern Culture
Mount Holyoke College
Tisch School of the Arts, New York University
University at Buffalo, State University of New York
University of North Carolina
University of Pennsylvania
Lewis Center for the Arts, Princeton University
Smith College
Symposium on Black Feminist History at Carter Woodson Institute for African-American Studies, University of Virginia
African American Studies Department, Yale University

How to See The Washing Society:

Scan here to see the film *The Washing Society*:

Distribution: Canyon Cinema, Film-Makers Cooperative, Canadian Filmmakers Distribution Centre, Kino Rebelde, Light Cone (Paris)
Streaming: Documentary Alliance DAFilms, Kanopy, Ovid, Prime Video, Projectr

EPILOGUE

Things change.

Our neighborhood laundromat where we used to wash our clothes isn't there anymore. It's been replaced by a new apartment complex.

Many of the city laundromats we visited have disappeared.

Atlantis Superwash

                                      New Lucky Laundromat

        Super Suds

                 Second Avenue Launderette

Now there is an app with a woman's name, not a she but an it.

A laundry service on your phone that picks up your clothes at 10:00pm,
in a truck that moves through the streets,
      across a bridge,
           to a catacomb of machines
that runs   all night.

And in this way, there are still two hands
or four
      or six
           or even twenty
probably more
washing your skirt, your shirt, your socks,
almost touching you
      almost connecting
           with your skin
another layer.

HAND BOOK

    You'll never see those hands
    (or the person they belong to).
    It's guaranteed.

    With the sunrise,
    your clothes return to you,
            minus the lint
                    left in the dryer,
    washed and folded.

contributors

Andrea Estepa ("Service Not Servitude") is a historian of women and social movements in the United States. As a Research Fellow in Reproductive Justice History and Popular Political Education at Smith College, she creates content for a website that traces the histories of women of color, low-income women, and queer women organizing for sexual and reproductive self-determination in the United States. She holds a PhD in US History and the History of Women and Gender from Rutgers University, and has taught at Oberlin, William and Mary, and Juniata College. She is the author of "When a 'Sister' Is a Mother: Maternal Thinking and Feminist Action, 1967–1980," published in *U.S. Women's History: Untangling the Threads of Sisterhood* (Rutgers, 2017) and "Taking the White Gloves Off: Women Strike for Peace and 'The Movement,' 1967–73," published in *Feminist Coalitions: Historical Perspectives on Second Wave Feminism in the United States* (Illinois, 2008).

Silvia Federici ("Foreword" and "Reflections on Laundry and Reproductive Labor: In Conversation with Silvia Federici") is a feminist scholar and activist. Her book, *Caliban and the Witch: Women, the Body, and Private Accumulation* (Autonomedia, 2004), investigates the rise of capitalism and its central subjugation of women's bodies, with an analysis of the role of the witch in relationship to colonialism, enslavement, and the modern state. In 1972, Federici co-founded the International Feminist Collective, which launched the Wages for Housework campaign. In the 1980s, she taught in Nigeria where she supported the struggles of students and teachers and was co-founder of the Committee for Academic Freedom in Africa. Federici is active in the anti-globalization and anti-death penalty movements in the United States. Her books include *Re-enchanting the World: Feminism and the Politics of the Commons* (PM Press, 2018) and *Beyond the Periphery of the Skin: Rethinking, Remaking, and Reclaiming the Body in Contemporary Capitalism* (PM Press, 2019). Federici's theory of reproductive labor is integral to a global, feminist analysis of capitalist accumulation, sex work, and the intimate labor of care.

Jasmine Holloway ("Taking on a Role") is an actor, singer, and writer who works to excavate the bones of a character before she can tell their story, honoring the life and times of the people she is portraying in a performance. Her New York theater credits include *Generations* at Soho Rep, and *The Wiz*, *In The Heights*, and *Tambourines To Glory* at Harlem Repertory Theatre. Holloway teaches theater at Brooklyn Charter School.

Tera W. Hunter ("A Hole in the History: In Conversation with Tera W. Hunter") is an historian and scholar of African-American studies, labor, gender, and race. In her first book *To 'Joy My Freedom: Southern Black Women's Lives and Labors after the Civil War* (Harvard, 1997), she traces the lives of newly emancipated black women and reveals the centrality of their work to the political and social struggles of late nineteenth-century southern American life. Hunter's book *Bound in Wedlock: Slave and Free Black Marriage in the Nineteenth Century* (Harvard, 2017) received numerous awards, including the Stone Book Award from the Museum of African American History. Hunter has also written many articles and essays on desegregation, diversity in education, and equity pedagogy. She is the co-author, with Robin D.G. Kelley and Earl Lewis, of *The Making of a People: A History of African-Americans* (forthcoming from W.W. Norton) and is the Edwards Professor of American History at Princeton University.

Amanda Katz ("Sound of a Machine Door Closing") is a film editor whose work has screened at Ann Arbor Film Festival, Encuentros del Otro Cine Festival Internacional de Cine Documental (Ecuador), Microscope Gallery, San Francisco International Film Festival, and UnionDocs. Katz holds an MFA in Integrated Media Arts from Hunter College, CUNY.

Mahoma López ("In Praxis: A Bridge Between Art and Activism") is a Mexican Latino who began his journey as a leader in the Hot & Crusty fast food workers' organizing campaign and served as president of its independent union. He went on to serve as the lead labor organizer for the Laundry Workers Center and is currently the Co-Executive Director, training workers to develop their skills and improve their working conditions.

Margarita Lopez ("A Thousand Pieces a Day") is a long-time Lower East Side resident and mother of two adult sons. Currently, she works as an administrative assistant in Manhattan. She appears in *The Washing Society*, where she is interviewed about her job in a laundromat.

Luo Xiaoyuan ("Finding the Stain: A Transcript in Translation") is a translator–interpreter and a journalist.

Lizzie Olesker (co-author and co-director) makes theater and performance, reflecting on the politics and poetry of everyday experience. Her most recent plays include *5 Stages of Grief*, *Night Shift*, and the collaborative *Language of Dolls*. Her work has been presented at Cherry Lane Theatre, Clubbed Thumb, Dixon Place, New Georges, Ohio Theater, and The Public

Theate. As an actor, she's performed with the Talking Band, at La Mama and Mabou Mines Theater. She's received support from Blue Mountain Center, Brooklyn Arts Council, Dramatists Guild, Hedgebrook, and the New York Foundation for the Arts. Olesker lives in Brooklyn and teaches playwriting at New York University and The New School.

Rosanna Rodríguez ("In Praxis: A Bridge Between Art and Activism") is the Co-Executive Director of the Laundry Workers Center where she strives to improve conditions for workers in the laundry, warehouse, and restaurant industries. Rodríguez has actively participated in more than thirteen worker-led organizing campaigns. She is a member of the Steering Committee of The Workers Institute at Cornell University, which engages in research and education on contemporary labor issues. Rodríguez attended law school at Universidad Autónoma de Santo Domingo in the Dominican Republic.

Emily Rubin ("Loads of Prose: From the Beginning") is a fiction writer and co-founder of Loads of Prose, a reading and performance series that takes place in laundromats around the country. Her novel *Stalina* (Mariner Books, 2011) received the Amazon Debut Novel Award, and she's been supported by the New York State Council on the Arts and the Sarah Verdone Writing Award. Her short stories and essays have appeared in *All the Restaurants in New York*, *Confrontation*, *Good Works Review*, *Ice Floe Press*, *Litbreak*, *Poets & Writers*, and *The Smart Set*. She founded the Write Treatment Workshops for cancer patients and survivors.

Lynne Sachs (co-author and co-director) is a filmmaker and poet. With each project, Sachs investigates the connection between the body, the camera, and the materiality of film itself. Embracing archives, found images, letters, and journals, her work enacts a critical journey through reality and memory. In films such as *The House of Science*, *Which Way is East*, *Your Day is My Night*, and *Film About a Father Who*, Sachs uses hybrid form and collaboration, incorporating documentary, performance, and collage. Retrospectives of Sachs's films have been presented at festivals in Argentina, China, Costa Rica, Cuba, Germany, Ireland, South Korea, and the UK, as well as on the Criterion Channel and at NYC's Museum of the Moving Image. In 2019, Tender Buttons Press published her collection *Year by Year: Poems*. *Lynne Sachs: Interviews* is forthcoming from The University Press of Mississippi as part of their Conversations with Filmmakers series. Sachs has received a Guggenheim Fellowship in the Arts and lives in Brooklyn.

Veraalba Santa ("Score for a Folding Dance") is a bilingual performer from Puerto Rico living in Brooklyn. Santa is interested in collecting images, objects, movements, behaviors, and texts, which she incorporates into her performances. Selected collaborations include working with Caborca Theater, Talking Band, Sally Silvers & Dancers, and Lynne Sachs (*Your Day is My Night*). Her choreography has been presented at Saint Marks Church,

La MaMa, Gibney Dance, the Hemispheric Institute in Buenos Aires, the Festival Ibero-Americano in Spain, and Ciego de Avila in Cuba.

Stephen Vitiello ("Shake, Rattle, and...") is a sound artist and electronic musician, creating site-specific installations, CDs/LPs, performances, and soundtracks for film, video, and dance. Over the last thirty years, he has collaborated extensively with visual artists such as Tony Oursler, Julie Mehretu, Joan Jonas, Lynne Sachs, and musicians, including Pauline Oliveros, Taylor Deupree, Steve Roden, Ryuichi Sakamoto, Scanner, and Brendan Canty (Fugazi). Vitiello has been awarded a Guggenheim Fellowship in the Arts, an Alpert/Ucross Award in Music, and a Creative Capital Award. He is currently chair of Kinetic Imaging at Virginia Commonwealth University.

LIST OF ILLUSTRATIONS

pp. xii–xiii: Ching Valdes-Aran in *Every Fold Matters* live performance at New Lucky Laundromat, Brooklyn. Photo by Lynne Sachs.

pp. 17–18: Lint and laundry cart dance from *The Washing Society* film. Photos by Sean Hanley.

p. 28: Margarita Lopez's hands folding in *The Washing Society*. Photos by Sean Hanley.

p. 30: Laundromat interiors in *The Washing Society*. Photos by Sean Hanley and Lynne Sachs.

pp. 35–36: IN MOTION — A Folding Dance. Jasmine Holloway, Veraalba Santa, and Ching Valdes-Aran in *Every Fold Matters* at New Lucky Laundromat. Photos by Lynne Sachs.

pp. 39–42: IN MOTION — Transforming through Clothing. Ching Valdes-Aran and Veraalba Santa in *The Washing Society*. Photos by Sean Hanley.

p. 45: Veraalba Santa and Ching Valdes-Aran in *Every Fold Matters* at The Tank, New York City. Photo by Lizzie Olesker and Lynne Sachs.

pp. 92–95: Lula Holloway in *The Washing Society*. Photos by Sean Hanley, Lizzie Olesker, and Lynne Sachs.

p. 98: Jasmine Holloway in *The Washing Society*. Photos by Sean Hanley.

pp. 99–112: Archival articles from *The Atlanta Constitution* (previously *The Daily Constitution*): "Arrest of Washerwomen," May 14, 1881, full page; "Washer Womens Strike," July 21, 1881; "The Doughty Women," July 26, 1881; "The Wet Clothes," July 29, 1881; "The Washerwomen," July 30, 1881; "The Washing Amazons," August 3, 1881.

pp. 117–18: IN MOTION — Lint with Voices. Images of lint with words accompanied by a soundtrack of two women speaking in Chinese and Spanish in *The Washing Society.* Photos by Sean Hanley.

p. 120: "Washing for Dignity and Safety on the Job," Laundry Workers Center poster.

p. 122: March and rally, Laundry Workers Center, Sunset Park, Brooklyn, 2019. Photo by Lynne Sachs.

p. 124: March and protest, Laundry Workers Center, East Harlem, 2018. Photo by Lynne Sachs.

pp. 127–28: IN MOTION — Dancing on Washing Machines. Veraalba Santa in Atlantis Super Wash, Brooklyn. Photos by Mark Street.

p. 129: Wing Hung Ho's hands counting coins in Broome Street Laundromat in *The Washing Society*. Photo by Sean Hanley.

p. 131: Looking through a glass door in *The Washing Society*. Photo by Sean Hanley.

pp. 132–33: IN MOTION — Two Women Folding. Brooklyn laundromat workers in *The Washing Society*. Photos by Lynne Sachs.

p. 135: Pillowcase sign in *The Washing Society.* Photo by Sean Hanley.

pp. 140–46: Wages for Housework 1970s campaign posters, flyers, and photo from the Silvia Federici Collection at the Feminist Theory Archive, Pembroke Center for Teaching and Research on Women, Brown University.

pp. 148–53: Close-ups of hair, lint, a sign, and the sky in *The Washing Society.* Photos by Sean Hanley.

p. 156: "Negro Laundress in Black and White, Rhode Island, 1902." Photo by Gertrude Kasebier, courtesy of the Shorpy American Historical Photo Archive.

pp. 161–62: Signs in laundromat windows. Photos by John Freyer.

p. 164: *Every Fold Matters* poster, designed by Sofía Gallisá Muriente.

p. 166: Veraalba Santa, Ching Valdes-Aran, and Jasmine Holloway in rehearsal. Photo by Lynne Sachs.

p. 168: Poster for *The Washing Society,* design by Rebecca Shapass with art by Cathy Daly.

p. 170–72: On set with cinematographer Sean Hanley, Ching Valdes-Aran, Jasmine Holloway, Veraalba Santa, and Tony Torn at Barclay Center and Bergen Street Laundromat, Brooklyn. Photos by Lizzie Olesker and Lynne Sachs.

p. 174: On set with Jasmine Holloway, Ching Valdes-Aran, and Veraalba Santa, Brooklyn. Photo by Lynne Sachs.

p. 177: Ching Valdes-Aran, New Lucky Laundromat. Photo by Lynne Sachs.

ACKNOWLEDGMENTS

Our cross-disciplinary project included the site-specific hybrid performance *Every Fold Matters* (2015–2017), the film *The Washing Society* (2018, 45 minutes), and now this book *Hand Book: A Manual on Performance, Process, and the Labor of Laundry*. We are grateful to many people who were an integral part of each phase of our project.

Every Fold Matters was produced by Emily Rubin (Loads of Prose) and developed with the actors Jasmine Holloway and Veraalba Santa, who each contributed writing to this collection. In addition, we want to recognize actors Ching Valdez-Aran and Tony Torn who were an essential part of the devising and performing. Andrew Tilson, director of the Workers Unite! Film Festival, was an enthusiastic supporter of the tour of these live performances in New York City. Beata Calińska was a behind-the-scenes force as lighting director and stage manager. Amanda Katz, also a contributor to this book, provided key audio-visual support from the top of a dryer during our shows, and later became our film's editor. Sean Hanley, as cinematographer, contributed to all of our moving images. His keen eye brings a profound sensitivity to the project in all of its iterations, including the photos in this book. Stephen Vitiello's delicate, expansive music and sound design were indispensable, and he recounts his process in this book.

Rob Kenter provided astute guidance and support early on for *Hand Book*. Translation is an essential part of our playscript. We turned to Ian Holloway for his expertise in Mandarin translation, and to Marichi Scharron for her nuanced understanding of spoken Spanish. Artist Abby Goldstein shared her innovative ideas on book design. Mafe Simonsen and Cate Fallon provided energetic production assistance. Dana Sachs gave sharp editorial feedback. Visionary co-directors Eileen A. Fradenburg Joy and Vincent W.J. van Gerven Oei of punctum books brought *Hand Book* into being. Eileen offered a close reading of our text which informed her incredibly sharp editorial insights. Vincent interpreted our writing and images through his exhilarating book design.

We thank the Brooklyn Arts Council, Fandor FIX Filmmakers Program, Lower Manhattan Cultural Council, New York State Council on the Arts, Puffin Foundation, The Tank, Women and Media Coalition, and Workers Unite! Film Festival for their support at various stages of the project. We also thank our hundreds of supporters who contributed to our two fund-raising campaigns for the making of our performance and film.

Throughout this ten-year collaboration, our partners Blaise Corrigan and Mark Street, and our now adult sons and daughters Harry, Mavis, and Abe Corrigan, and Maya and Noa Street-Sachs have been steadfastly there for us.

www.ingramcontent.com/pod-product-compliance
Lightning Source LLC
Chambersburg PA
CBHW081209170426
43198CB00018B/2902